THROUGH
THE
GATE

THE STRATEGY FOR REACHING THE UNCHURCHED

MARC PRITCHETT

Foreword by
Dr. Johnny Hunt

WESTBOW
PRESS®
A DIVISION OF THOMAS NELSON
& ZONDERVAN

WestBow Press books may be ordered through booksellers or by contacting:

WestBow Press
A Division of Thomas Nelson & Zondervan
1663 Liberty Drive
Bloomington, IN 47403
www.westbowpress.com
844-714-3454

ISBN: 978-1-6642-4969-1 (sc)
ISBN: 978-1-6642-4968-4 (hc)
ISBN: 978-1-6642-4970-7 (e)

Library of Congress Control Number: 2021923179

Printed in the United States of America.

WestBow Press rev. date: 04/08/2022

CONTENTS

ACKNOWLEDGMENTS

To my best friend, my wife, Stephanie. Thank you for always putting up with my crazy hours, for my crazy ideas (which I call vision), and most of all, for always walking with me in this life. When we were just kids, you told me you wanted to grow old with me. Well, honey, we're off to a great start! I love your heart for Jesus and your sense of discernment. You always inspire me to strive to be the best man I can be for you and for my Lord. I am truly blessed with the most compassionate, passionate, and gifted woman of God I know. You are the greatest wife, mother, grandmother, and because of you, our ministry exists! You are truly one of a kind, and you deserve only the best. I am so thankful we get to do life together. I can't wait to see what the next 32 years will be - You are truly the epitome of the "Proverbs 31 woman":

> Strength and honor are her clothing; She shall rejoice in time to come. She opens her mouth with wisdom, And on her tongue is the law of kindness. Charm is deceitful and beauty is passing, But a woman who fears the Lord, she shall be praised. (Proverbs 31:25–26, 30, NKJV)

To my son, Tyler. You've followed me every step since you could walk, and today, I see you taking lead in so many areas. And honestly, you do it better than I ever could. You and Maggie are so special to your mom and me. And the three grands (Beckham, Kanon, and Jillian) are the parts of you we love the most (you'll get it one day!) I am so proud of you. I love you, buddy!

To my baby girl, Ashli Marie. You are beyond a daddy's girl. You are so very precious to me, and you'll always be my princess. You and Keith are such amazingly talented, anointed, and passionate worship leaders, I love going into the Throne Room under your leadership! And most of all, when you gave me that little granddaughter, Ember Rose, I felt like I got to raise you all over again. Oh, how I adore that little girl! And most recently, my grandson Braven—he is so special. I love you!

To my mom, Jennifer. What can I say? You've always cheered me on and believed in me—perhaps when others wouldn't have. I've always felt like I could do anything I put my mind to, and for that I honor you. I know that's what moms are for, but you excel them all! Thank you for always being there and showing me the way. I love you!

To my dad, Bill (in heaven). You have finished your course here on earth, but your investment in me as a young boy, and even in my adulthood, has molded me into the man I am today. I can never thank you enough for the life lessons, the hunts, the ballgames, and most of all, seeing you fall and get back up! The last fifteen years of your life were my best with you because I saw the real you—a man who was passionate for God and His people! I can't wait to see you in heaven. I love you!

To Rick and Linda, you are like my second parents! I can say for sure I would not be where I am today without you. Thank you for your wisdom, your support, and constant love. I love you both!

To Tracy Brock, you are the truest of friends! You are much more than an office manager, you are family. Thank you for all you do, we could not do this without you!

To my church family, NorthRidge Church of Thomaston. You guys have inspired me to believe God even more than I thought possible! Your devotion and hunger for the Word, for God, and His people make me want to become better. I believe our best years are still ahead as we seek to reach our community and the world for Jesus.

To my pastoral staff, David and Kathryn Maguire, Tyler and Maggie Pritchett, Keith and Ashli Dunn, and Cody and Hannah Knight. You guys are top shelf, the best of the best! I could not, nor would I want to, do this thing without you. I love our mantra: "The best idea wins." That's what make us work.

To our deacons and board of stewards. Thank you from the bottom of my heart for believing in the God in me and for your counsel to help make us the best church we can be in Christ. I love and respect you more than words can express.

To the RUSH Board. I am so thankful for each of you more than you'll ever know. Doug and Starla, your friendship, guidance, partnership, and love have inspired me to pay attention to detail. We could not do it without you. Steve and Stacy Richardson, your love and belief in me—even when I didn't believe in myself—has kept the RUSH motor running strong. Your partnership in RUSH has enabled us to reached thousands of people at our events and abroad. I love you dearly! Josh and Amanda Rhye, I am so thankful for your ministry and pastoral approach to everything we do. Josh, every time we are faced with a challenge, your spiritual insight offers me solace and confidence the more in my God. I love you Brother!

Ben and Shelley Daniel, you were the first I asked to sit on the board, and I am forever grateful. Your creativity and solid logistical gifting have brought many a chaotic moment together famously. I love you! David and Kathryn Maguire, I am so grateful for your ever-constant enthusiasm. Your ideas are paramount to our success and your friendship means the world to me. I love you! Tommy and Julie Ford, thank you for the solid advice and consistency in everything we do! You are an integral part, bringing your business savvy into the mix, and your servant's heart is beyond any I have ever seen. You are family, but you are my friend. I love you dearly! Scott and Nancy Presutti, some of us still think you are in the secret service! Everything you do is with excellence and a heart of service, and you do it so gracefully. I love you both! Tyler and Maggie, what can I say? Your creativity, and administrative gifting is second to none. I watched you grow into a masterful leader. Love you both! Ashli and Keith, you are gifted beyond your own understanding. I am so thankful for your wisdom and heart for ministry…It's truly beyond any I have seen before. I love you!

To our many RUSH partners and iServe team. I say it all the time: you are the truest heroes in my book! You give selflessly of your time, your hearts, your finances, and your gifts to help us reach this generation for Jesus. Each of you are so very special to Stephanie and me, and we consider you a part of our family! There will be a line in heaven waiting to say "thank you" for spreading the message of hope to the world. Thank you for reaching through the gate. I love you all dearly!

Mostly, to my Lord and Savior Jesus Christ, for Your relentless pursuit of my life. I must have told you "no" a dozen times, yet You persisted! You are the lover of my soul and the One I love the most. You have pulled me out more times than I can count, and when I was all alone, hopeless, helpless, prideful, broken, undone, and unlovable, You loved me still. My heart, my soul, my life, and all the glory belongs to You! I love You, Jesus!

> He that dwelleth in the secret place of the most
> High shall abide under the shadow of the Almighty.
> (Psalm 91:1, KJV)

FOREWORD, BY DR. JOHNNY HUNT

I love to read stories of where an individual declares that which they first received in miraculous order, which God then takes and uses to write His story. As you read *Through the Gate,* I believe you will see how God can take an individual's life and literally give them a new identity, and with it a new purpose in life. I have always believed that apart from a personal encounter with Jesus Christ, I would never know the purpose for which I was born in the first place.

I love real-life stories, not theories. I like to read the story behind someone who has had a divine intervention and a divine execution of something God has done in their heart and pulled out of their life as they were working out their own salvation.

It all began as Marc was introduced to orphan ministry. It was then that he viewed it more personally, through the eyes of faith, and saw that this was what really happened to him. God had chosen to adopt him and his family. His change that God brought led to the change of so many others. Too many seem to be deaf to the call of God in Isaiah 6. In this great biblical truth, God makes it clear that He is calling out the called and we need to say more often, "Here am I. Send me."

Here is a book that invites us to join Him on this journey, even as we think of orphans. In some countries, we are noted as outcasts at the gate. We liken them to those, even in our own world, who are outside of relationship with God—not yet saved, never allowing Christ to redeem them as they turn from their sins and place their faith in Christ. One thing this book will help all of us do is to see others as they are, but see, through the eye of faith, what they could become.

Here is a message that is single-minded, single-purposed, and single-hearted. Tell your story of your failures, not just your successes, and see how God takes that vulnerable life and draws others to join you on your journey. Here is a book you can use right now —and by the way, none of us are promised tomorrow. This life of reaching others, this life of making His life known, is truly tough, but it is worth it. One of the first Christian songs I learned was "It Will Be Worth It All When We See Christ." I trust you will not only read this book, *Through the Gate*, but you will pass it on to friends.

Marc, thank you for giving your life to Him and then sharing His life through you.

Johnny Hunt is Senior Vice President of Evangelism and Pastoral Leadership, North American Mission Board. He is also the former Southern Baptist Convention president, 2008–2010 and Pastor Emeritus First Baptist Church Woodstock, GA, after serving thirty-three years.

INTRODUCTION

I have had many close friends over the past several years ask me, "Marc, when will you write a book on your ministry model, RUSH. When will you tell the story?" So, after much prayer (and a little procrastination), here it goes.

Rather than writing and asking you, the reader, to learn, why don't we simply agree to take this journey together. I say "journey" since I, for one, appreciate an author who realizes he or she has not cornered the market on any given subject. Rather than describing in detail all that I have learned in my illustrious career as a leader (see how pious that sounds!), let's just share what good and bad we have learned along the way—and maybe even the learning that lies ahead. I do believe we each have something profound to say about ministry and how our life may have impacted the world. My hope in writing this book is to divulge some of the good and highlight the ugly so that you may glean some valuable insights in your own work for the Lord.

My experience is not predicated solely on ministry but includes my childhood, my marriage, my children, my time in the military, as well as ministry abroad. I believe it's the whole of our life experiences that tells the greatest story. Oftentimes, we share our life experience and knowledge by looking through a limited scope—let's say, the last five years. But when I look at my life today as a pastor, speaker, father, husband, and grandfather (the grands call me "G"), I must take into account the entirety of my life. Scripture teaches, "As a man thinks in his heart, so is he" (Proverbs 23:7a, NKJV), thus leading me to understand how we see things the way we do. The reality for me is that I am who I am and I believe what I believe, based on the sum total of my life thus far. And the same is true for you!

In fact, I believe we each offer great insight into areas in which we have experience. My dear wife and best friend, Stephanie—says it this way: "You can't take someone where you've never been." This statement is both elementary and paramount to understanding ministry and to reaching the unchurched world for Jesus. Before you can make others "hunger and thirst after righteousness" (Matthew 5:6, KJV), they will need to see you feasting on God, His wonder, and renown!

Perhaps the main reason that many today reject the invitation to attend a local church is they do not see many in the church feasting on God. It seems as if the church is becoming more unappealing to many, especially millennials. Perhaps, we have been sold a bill of goods that has led us to feast on programs, music, the newest lighting scheme, cool, catchy sermon series, and so on. Don't get me wrong—there is absolutely nothing wrong with those things! They are incredibly beneficial. I even use them to my benefit. But they cannot replace the authentic move of God and the power of the Holy Spirit's drawing of lost sinners, as the Man of God breaks the bread of life. That's what changes people. That's what reaches the ones far from God. Subsequently, the person who has come face to face with his bankrupt condition and been changed forever by the touch of Jesus is the one who will change the world. That's the person who can bring someone Christ. That's what we have to see in the Church—undisputable life change.

I have seen the unchurched, the orphaned, the least of these, if you will. I have identified them and can still see their faces pressed through the bars of the gate. I will explain this in detail in chapter 1. Regardless of where you are in your life, whether a pastor, a leader, a layperson, or even someone who feels you've completely failed at life, God can use you and your story to reach *the unchurched*. God doesn't need your strengths. If you are reading this thinking that God couldn't use you to reach the lost, then you are just the one *HE can use*. In fact, recently, I heard a pastor say, "If you graduated top of your class and were voted Most Likely to Succeed, there's hope even for you!" You see, it is in our weaknesses that "God's strength is made perfect" (2 Corinthians 12:9, KJV). When you allow God to use you and your shortcomings, He gets all the credit. And quite frankly, God would have it no other way. It's in my weakness that God has my full attention to speak truth and purpose into my life. And it's in those moments that I hear Him, I respond, and lives are changed!

As it relates to this truth, perhaps the greatest word the Lord gave me came about a year ago, when a good friend in the ministry admitted to an affair, which shattered his ministry and many people around him. As I was speaking to him, I told him that the Lord would still use him "in spite of" his bad decision. The Lord quickened my spirit, and before I could even finish my statement, I said, "No, I take that back! If you will accept this season of learning and repentance, the Lord will use you *because of* your bad decision." I will also address this later in the book.

Therefore, I write this book realizing that in and of myself, I can help no one. I can offer no answers to life's dilemmas. I offer no quick fix, only real-life applications. I only know what God has allowed me to see and learn through my own walk. It has not all been easy. In fact, quite the opposite! Walking with Jesus in this life is likely the most difficult thing you'll ever do. So, it is with fear and trembling that I take this journey with you. I will share my thoughts, my heart, and even some personal experiences as we seek to uncover some deliberate steps to reach *Through the Gate* and touch the lives of the *unchurched* world, for His glory!

This strategy is a friendly reminder to us all that we are never really growing our church until we reach the unchurched. Many a church today "grows" by the losses by attrition of another church. But if that's all we do, we are merely operating a revolving door where we are losing people at the same rate as we are reaching them. *I, for one, do not wish to "grow" a ministry containing unhappy church members who are looking for the next best thing.* In fact, most seasoned pastors will attest that pleasing the unhappy churchgoer, who has not made peace with his or her previous church, is quite the challenge. Friend, let me be the first to say: that is why this strategy is needed! Let us go out and "reach" the unchurched, the orphaned, the world—those who stand outside the proverbial gate, in whom no one has invested. That's my mission. That is God's heart! Let's reach into our own community, our own backyard, and reach the people no one else is reaching. That is true evangelism.

In the following pages of this book, I have included eight simple principles to reach *Through the Gate* into the lives of the unchurched community, the spiritually orphaned. Let us join the ranks of those great men and women of God who have answered God's call to ministry. Let's go reach the world!

1

WHO WILL GO?

We've all heard missionaries, pastors, and leaders charge a congregation to accept the great commission, asking almost with a sense of urgency, "Who will go?" The appeal sounds out, and the altars fill with prospective missionaries who wish to follow in the footsteps of great missionaries like Hudson Taylor, William Carey, Lottie Moon, and, more recently, Jim Elliot and Nate Saint. But if we miss the origin of this great question, we miss the fuel behind it, which could greater ignite our passion not only to "go" but to "keep going"!

This question is actually a passage, a dialogue, found in the book of Isaiah. But despite hearing or reading this passage, many have never read the text in its entirety. As any great seminary student will tell you, the three most important considerations in reading a Biblical passage are as follows (in no particular order):

- context
- context
- context

To place a passage in its proper context, you must consider the entire thought by reading what lies before and after the passage, who is speaking, to whom it is being spoken, and the cultural milieu at the time the passage was spoken. The well-known passage from Isaiah 6 reads as follows:

> In the year that King Uzziah died, I saw the Lord sitting on a throne, high and lifted up, and the train of His robe filled the temple. Above it stood seraphim; each one had six wings: with two he covered his face, with two he covered his feet, and with two he flew. And one cried to another and said: "Holy, holy, holy is the Lord of hosts; The whole earth is full of His glory!" And the posts of the door were shaken by the voice of him who cried out, and the house was filled with smoke. So I said: "Woe is me, for I am undone! Because I am a man of unclean lips, And I dwell in the midst of a people of unclean lips; For my eyes have seen the King, The Lord of hosts." Then one of the seraphim flew to me, having in his hand a live coal which he had taken with the tongs from the altar. And he touched my mouth with it, and said: "Behold, this has touched your lips; Your iniquity is taken away, And your sin purged." *Also I heard the voice of the Lord, saying: "Whom shall I send, And who will go for Us?" Then I said, "Here am I! Send me."* (Isaiah 6:1–8, KJV, emphasis added)

So, in context, this question is one of divine origin from Jehovah God, the Creator, and redeemer of the world, to the humble servant, the prince of the prophets, the prophet Isaiah. Without elaborating for days on this passage (which I am tempted to do), this question comes immediately following Isaiah "seeing" in a vision, the Shekinah Glory of the Lord. Not only has he seen the glory and majesty of God, but in light of that glory, Isaiah has seen his own filthiness, as he states, "Woe is me, for I am undone! Because I am a man of unclean lips, and dwell in the midst of a people of unclean lips" (v. 5). But if seeing God's glory weren't enough, one of the Seraphim flew over and touched his lips with a fiery coal, which speaks of the fire on the altar of sacrifice, pointing of course to Jesus, the ultimate sacrifice for our sin. The Seraphim touches his lips and says, "Your iniquity is taken away … and your sin purged."

Then came the question from the Lord: "Whom shall I send …?" to which Isaiah replies, "Here am I! Send me" (v. 8).

So, in context, one can see why the prophet spoke so directly in his answer, as if to be standing among thousands of other prophets, shouting aloud like a child volunteering for the *greatest opportunity* he'd ever heard:

"Choose me!"

"I want to go!"

"Hey, over here. Pick me, pick me!"

And that is exactly the way it should unfold in our lives! As people who have been bought from the bonds of sin and shame, we should be standing in the proverbial line, anxiously awaiting the opportunity to go! The response by the great prophet came only after seeing himself in light of God's glory! Why, then, do we ponder for days, months, years, or longer with the same question, as if to say, "Why should I go?" or "Why should I tell anyone anything?" or "Let someone else go"? Maybe, we too just need to see God's glory!

In 2004, while speaking at an international youth conference in the Caribbean, I was confronted with the same question: "Marc, will you go for me? Will you go for those *outside* the gate?" And on that day, I saw the glory of the Lord in a place I would have never thought to look. Allow me to lay the framework for this pivotal moment in my life.

There I was, the keynote speaker at a student conference where more than ten island nations were represented. The hour came for me to make my grand entrance to the main session, where all the students and leaders had gathered, each one anticipating the conference kickoff. As I made my way out of the less-than-hospitable living quarters, I walked past the main gate, where eight young orphans stood. Picture if you will their faces pressed partly through the gate's bars, as if imprisoned in a jail cell. The side on which they stood represented everything Jesus died for, the filth of the world, those "undone and with unclean lips" (v. 5). The side on which I stood represented the answer to all their life's questions. The conference center had been situated in one of the foulest neighborhoods in the city, surrounded by large cinderblock walls with broken pieces of glass carefully situated atop the wall and firmly planted in dried mortar. The scene was reminiscent of a military compound surrounded with rolls of barbed concertina wire, which layered the wall's crest. Why was the place so fortified? I remember thinking, *What are we protecting?* or, perhaps more accurately, *What are we being protected from?* Why did we want to keep some people out while making others most welcome? The truth revealed on that day would forever change my life!

As I made my way past the orphan boys, I rather flippantly asked the conference director, who was escorting me to the conference hall, "What about those kids? Can we let them come into the session too?"

I can still hear her simple yet haunting response. "Well, *those kids* can't come in. They are not the kind you would want in here with us. They are street kids." Though I was shocked by her calloused response, I did what any guest speaker would do—nothing! After all, I was her guest, in her country, and I was in no place to rebuke her for the brash perception of the lost and undone in her community. I digressed and proceeded to make my way to the main session, still thinking of the boys outside the gate. I preached the message, gave an invitation, and lives were changed, mostly my own!

You see, while I preached in this nice building with the only air-conditioned room for miles, I was thinking of the ones on the outside looking in! Don't misunderstand me here. I cared greatly about the students in the conference. But I couldn't shake the image in my head of those orphaned boys outside the gate, and the words of the lady saying, "They are not the kind you want." The only problem was, they *were* the kind I wanted! And moreover, they were the exact kind Jesus died for! At that moment, long before I heard the term, *those orphan boys* became the epitome of the *unchurched* people group, the world on the outside. I will discuss the unchurched and who they are in greater detail in chapter 2.

Immediately following the session, I proceeded to the large rusty gate only to find *five* of the original eight boys still standing, faces still pressing through the bars. As I approached the gate, I observed a thick chain wrapped several times through the gate bars, held secure by a large padlock. By now, my sadness was turning to outright weeping as I came closer to the unwanted boys. I knelt down to look them directly in the eyes. I reached through the gate bars and grabbed the hand of the first child I could, then another, until each dirty, calloused hand was in mine. For some strange reason, they were each eagerly reaching for me as if I had something they wanted. I'm sure they thought I was crazy, because at this point, I was crying almost uncontrollably. I held their rough little hands for what seemed like an hour. Each one patiently waited for his or her turn to touch me, shake my hand, and give me a high five, a universal sign of friendship. Why were they so eager to touch me? Did they view me as the "man of God" with whom they hoped to connect? I didn't feel like a man of God but rather a man who chose not to "speak up for those who have no voice" when it counted the most (Proverbs 31:8, NLT). The truth is, it was me who was waiting to touch *them*, five orphans about to be adopted by Abba Father!

I should have fought harder to offer them a seat at the table. Had I failed miserably, or was God doing something bigger than just the one service? I wasn't sure. My spiritual lament for their souls must have been seen by every angel in heaven. I was truly burdened for them to repent and come to know Jesus! For a brief moment, I must have felt a very small part of what Jesus felt when the children were pressing in to touch him. The disciples responded much as the conference leader had responded to me. "Don't touch the master," they said, as if to say, "You're not worthy to touch Him." But Jesus's response was one of disdain and rebuke.

> But Jesus said, "Let the children come to me and do not hinder them! For the Kingdom of Heaven belongs to those who are like these children." (Matthew 19:14, NLT)

In that moment, I was repulsed by the lack of love, compassion, and interest many have for the physically orphaned (a.k.a., street kids). What happened next would launch my life on a trajectory to reach the unchurched with an unfailing passion. And I haven't yet reached my destination!

I continued to share Jesus with them and gave them the missionary's signature "sweetie," a pack of SweeTarts. Then, after a half hour of ministering to them, each one, realizing how important he was in God's sight, smiled and asked Jesus into his life! *I had just seen the Glory of the Lord* as it filled—not the temple, not the church, not the main session room, not my eloquent words within my three-point sermon, but in the lives of five young boys, and all *through the gate*, a locked gate nonetheless! In fact, had I unlocked an even bigger gate, a gate to the unchurched world at large, the ones I would spend my life trying to reach? You see, at that moment, I, like Isaiah, saw my dirt, my shame, my small mind, my feeble vision, in contrast to the Lord's vastness. As I look back now, it was as if the Lord spoke to me and said, "Who shall I send. Will you go for us—for the orphaned? Who will reach *Through the Gate?*"

To which I responded without a moment's hesitation, "Send me, Lord. I will go!"

God spoke to me and in such a sweet, still, small voice. He said, "Marc, when I found you, you too were outside the gate. It is where I meet every one of my precious children, on the outside."

What a metaphor! That's exactly the way it looked when Jesus rescued me. He reached *through the gate* of separation and brought me into a loving, secure relationship on the inside of Himself. I then understood why God brought me to that place and allowed me to cross paths with those precious boys. He revealed to me the true heartbeat of the Gospel and the drive behind the Great Commission. We were *all* orphaned before God adopted us as His own. And as you read this book, it will do you good to see yourself in that same light. We were all on the outside of the locked gate of redemption. No way in. No one to let us pass through. Perhaps even unwanted by some. But Jesus left His perfect throne in heaven and stepped into this dirty, undone world to reach through the gate of our depravity, to adopt us as His own! How, then, can we possibly build a church without extending a hand through the gates of indifference to reach the orphaned for Jesus? We can't.

With this newfound perception, the remainder of the conference was uniquely powerful, and we began ministering outside the gates in spontaneous street evangelism. After my encounter, I wanted to expose our team to the needs beyond the gates, and that day, God initiated in me a pursuit of the lost, with a level of intensity we all experienced that day.

This epic moment in my ministry changed my life. *I had embarked on my life's mission to reach the world, one orphaned life at a time!* The mission would reach beyond the physically orphaned and would reach into the lives of the spiritually orphaned, everyone outside the gate!

Just moments after the plane took off headed back home to Atlanta, my team either fast asleep or resting, God prompted me to take out a pen and write. Since I had spent many years in the military, I was forever using acronyms to shorten thoughts, phrases, titles, and so on, to drive home a point I could easily remember. I begin to write the words:

> a sense of urgency
> now is the time
> unsaved

> reaching out
>
> orphans

Before long, I had filled the napkin upon which I was writing. I finally wrote down the letters "R.U.S.H." and thought first of the great band with arguably the best drummer on the planet, Neil Peart. I then thought of reaching the orphans through the gate, both the real and the spiritually orphaned, with a sense of purpose and urgency. The result was *Reaching Unchurched Students for HIM*. The RUSH strategy was born—but not by my hands! It was those *outside the gate* who became the epicenter, the poster children for the unchurched. You see, I reached only five of the eight boys that day. I praise God for His grace (five is the number for grace in Scripture) in leading the five young boys to Jesus. But the three who left before I returned to share the Gospel, they were the ones I never forgot!

Where are they today? God only knows. I pray daily they found that blessed hope, even if I did not share it with them that day. But because of the missed opportunity to reach those three, I have intentionally set my sights on everything those three precious boys represent—the ones on the outside, the unchurched, the ones who walked away from the gate, the unwelcomed, unredeemed, unwanted, and unadopted, the literal and spiritual orphaned of this world!

I pray that after reading this book, you will be more apt to reach out with this same sense of urgency, to the unchurched, to the world! They may not be standing with their faces pressed against the stained-glass windows of your church. But make no mistake about it—they exist! Just look around you. They come in different packages. Some are poor, some are rich, some dirty, and yet others are clean. But each one is a spiritual orphan. You can't just look at them on the outside; you must also be intentional to see who they are on the inside. After all, if we are completely honest, we tend to seek after the people we want to come to our church. In fact, we want *all* people to come, but we expect them to look like, dress like, smell like, and worship like we do! If not, we respond just like the conference host: "They are not the kind we want in here." God help us never to forget what we were before we were adopted by God.

You may actually have to change your course of action, your mission statement, and ultimately your agenda. And go after them all, no matter who they are in the present. So, with that mandate, God still presses the question that demands your response: "Will you go?"

2

TAKE A LOOK AT YOU!

In the changing of your mission, or at least your angle, looking at yourself can be an interesting proposition—not only looking intently but realizing the areas of your shortcomings and fine-tuning them. The apostle Paul said, "But let each man examine himself" (1 Corinthians 11:28, KJV). I know what you're thinking. "Now, wait just a dog-gone minute! I have no problem examining your life, but my life? That's treading on thin ice. I would much rather *examine* you or anyone, for that matter! But you're asking me to look at me?" I am! And let me forewarn you, you might not like what you find.

In one of my favorite passages, Psalm 139, David wrote,

> O LORD, You have searched me and known me. You know my sitting down and my rising up; You understand my thought afar off. You comprehend my path and my lying down, And are acquainted with all my ways. For there is not a word on my tongue, But behold, O LORD, You know it altogether. You have hedged me behind and before, And laid Your hand upon me. Such knowledge is too wonderful for me; It is high, I cannot attain it. "Where can I go from Your Spirit? Or where can I

flee from Your presence?" If I ascend into heaven, You are there; If I make my bed in hell, behold, You are there. If I take the wings of the morning, And dwell in the uttermost parts of the sea, Even there Your hand shall lead me, And Your right hand shall hold me. If I say, "Surely the darkness shall fall on me," Even the night shall be light about me; Indeed, the darkness shall not hide from You, But the night shines as the day; The darkness and the light are both alike to You. For You formed my inward parts; You covered me in my mother's womb. I will praise You, for I am fearfully and wonderfully made; Marvelous are Your works, And that my soul knows very well. My frame was not hidden from You, When I was made in secret, And skillfully wrought in the lowest parts of the earth. Your eyes saw my substance, being yet unformed. And in Your book they all were written, The days fashioned for me, When as yet there were none of them. How precious also are Your thoughts to me, O God! How great is the sum of them! If I should count them, they would be more in number than the sand; When I awake, I am still with You." (Psalms 139:1–18 NKJV)

The first few times I read Psalm 139, it did not occur to me how many different ways David stated that God "knew" every corner of his life. Yet at the conclusion of twenty-two verses of the Psalmist speaking of God's sovereignty, he ends with "Search me oh God." Why is that? Why would the Psalmist be so redundant? What would cause such an eloquent writer as David to state an obvious contradiction or overstatement? After all, how many ways can one say that God has fully known me only to end that thought with "search me ... know me ..."? Were all the previous verses just glorious rhetoric? No. *There is a profound difference between God "knowing" every aspect of your life and you "granting" Him full access to it!*

So, let's get personal. How many times have you said to God, "This is what I want for my ministry? This is how much time, effort, and money I am willing to spend to get it. And, oh yeah, God, I'll throw you a bone every now and again too!"

Maybe you didn't say it exactly in the way, but the implication was there. However, when you truly apply the words of the Psalmist—"Search me Oh God, know my heart, try me … and see if there be in wickedness in me" (Psalm 139:23–24, NKJV)—that tends to invite a different perspective. Ministry begins to look different for you. The sense of urgency to "go" will forever channel your life decisions. Why? Because you have allowed God to probe within every facet of your being, even the private recesses that drive you to do what you do. What would happen if we got on our knees and cried out, "Any time, any place, any people, at any cost, send me, Lord. I'll go *through the gate*"? I'll tell you what would happen. We would see another Great Awakening, a harvest of souls, and a power within the Body that would drive us even the more to the lost. It is plausible.

Remember, it's not God's plan for us to "fix" everyone else. That's what He does through the Holy Spirit. Why, then, is it so easy to see everyone else's faults and shortcomings but not so easy to see our own? Simply put, if we acknowledge our own inefficiencies, we are forced to see that we are part of the problem in this crazy world—and then we are prompted to do something about it! In fact, although we might not say what the conference leader said to me—"You don't want those kids in your church"—we do say it with our actions!

I heard of a church that hosts a large mission advance once a year to promote missions in the community and abroad. It has become a pep rally of sorts for the church. Each year, they bring in missionaries from all around the globe and have them share the specific need for more missionaries and efforts in their land. Throughout the course of the week-long conference, many church members become motivated and often formulate plans to reach out in their own community. After all, even evangelism and talks of reaching the world magnetically prompt us all. One year in particular, someone was so prompted that he developed a flyer, and at the end of the flyer, he listed the church service times, with a big "We want to see you at church this Sunday" right in the center of the flyer. The church leadership saw the man's flyer, called a meeting, and forced him to drop the service times and, more importantly, the phrase. When asked why, they responded, "We don't want the wrong person to pick this flyer up. There's no telling what kind of people we'd have walk in here on Sunday!" And if we're really honest, and though it sounds completely despicable, it's a truth applied by many churches. Some are just better at not saying it so directly. God help us!

At the time I spoke at this conference, I had been a student pastor for just two years. I was too "unlearned" to know I was supposed to reach only the kind of people the church "wanted." Shortly after the conference, I was getting invitations to speak in other churches and abroad. But as a young pastor who seemed to have it all together, it was easy to see other peoples' problems and address them in a nicely wrapped sermonette with a Jesus bow on top. However, when I walked by the gate that day, everything I thought I knew about ministry changed. You see, when I looked at the orphans *through the gate*, I saw me! I saw who I used to be, the one standing in the prison of this world, trapped without a hope, just waiting for someone *real* to walk by, someone to see me through the gate. I also saw who I had become—the one with the answer to all of life's questions, because I now had Jesus and had been called to proclaim His glorious message to the world! Unfortunately, until I looked at me, the preacher, in light of those kids and the lost world, I was living in a fantasy world filled with arbitrary sermon titles and going from conference to conference. I realized God knew my heart full well when He called me, but I wasn't at the point of allowing Him into every facet of *my* life's work, at least not yet. I wasn't ready to say, as the Psalmist had, "Search me, oh God." I had a predetermined whitewashed idea of how it all was supposed to look and, better yet, how it all needed to unfold.

How many of us are doing that same thing right now? We are "serving" the Lord but doing so on our own terms, to fill in our own, albeit well-intended, agendas. We have decided who we will lead, the targeted demographic we will reach, and the ones we are certain we'll leave out. And when we write our prefab, Googled mission statements, we merely omit an entire group of people we are willing to leave out of the Kingdom. Jesus called them "the least of these." It is as if we are saying, "We want to take the message to the world, as long as the 'world' we reach looks, acts, worships, and believes like us." Jesus, however, took a different approach, didn't He?

In Matthew's Gospel, he stated,

> For I was hungry and you gave Me food; I was thirsty and you gave Me drink; I was a stranger and you took Me in; I was naked and you clothed Me; I was sick and you visited Me; I was in prison and you came to Me. (Matthew 25:35–36, NKJV).

His disciples were perplexed by such an assertion! After all, they had not seen Jesus in need of food, water, or clothing. They had not seen Him a stranger, a prison inmate, or even a sick person. Then Jesus dropped the bombshell ideology, with a profound teaching moment: "Assuredly, I say to you, inasmuch as you did it to one of the least of these My brethren, you did it to Me" (v.40).

What was Jesus saying to His followers? After the mic drop, He issued a divine mandate for us to open our eyes, our hearts, and our pocketbooks and to show compassion to the ones outside the gate, the "least of these."

In fact, I may not have been physically orphaned, hungry, naked, or in prison, but most of my life exemplified that in a spiritual light. I was outside the gate looking in, and through the ebb and flow of life's chance and God's Divine plan, I was redeemed and was called to be a pastor! And then it began.

"Marc Pritchett, you're a preacher?"

I wish I could tell you how many times I heard that same statement from people who knew me *before* becoming a Christian. Ironically, the same could said of you: "_____ [put your name here]. You're a Christian!" The truth is, God really can use the "foolishness of this world to confound the wise" (1 Corinthians 1:27, KJV).

I'm evidence of that. He can use anyone. He uses me, and He can even use *you*! That day on the return fight to Atlanta, I prayed the prayer of David:

> Search me, O God, and know my heart: try me, and know my thoughts: And see if there be any wicked way in me, and lead me in the way everlasting. (Psalm 139:23–24, NKJV)

What He revealed to me that day changed the direction of my life forever. I began to reflect on where I had been prior to my relationship with King Jesus. I had humble beginnings as a small-town boy, with a father who was a millworker and a stay-at-home mom, directing traffic in school zones. She was the bomb! She dressed in a quintessential police-lady uniform—orange gloves, hat, and the coolest whistle! I have an older sister, Michele, who to this day introduces me as her "older brother." She is in obvious denial. As you can see, it was dysfunction from the word go.

I was an average student with tremendous potential who got by mostly by being the class clown. Some teachers loved me, while others—well, let's just say, not so much. I loved making people laugh and would stop at nothing to send the class into a whirlwind of laughter. At times, I would even use less popular kids as the subjects of my jokes, to make people laugh. But in the light of God having "searched me and known me," I saw everything and everyone through a different lens. I must pause here to say that if I ever hurt anyone reading this book, please forgive me. There was no excuse for my behavior. I was simply acting out to placate my own low self-esteem. I just covered it up well. I am sure many of you can relate to being on either the giving or the receiving end of such conduct. The reality is that both parties lose out by not getting to know people and failing to establish authentic relationships. Imagine the people you treated unfairly in life, perhaps in middle school, who you never befriended as a result. I am sure I missed out on some amazing relationships due to my own lack of self-awareness. If you are a student reading this book right now, this is a good time to take inventory of your life and look at what pain you may have brought into another person's life. It may not be too late to undo some of the wrong you've caused in another.

Bullying has risen to an unprecedented high and is no longer limited to in-person interactions but now includes online harassment. Remember, Psalm 139 forces you to see yourself as God sees you, not as you want to be seen. Take time not only to notice people but time to engage them. A smile or a kind word may spark a friendship that will change the course of history for the glory of God forever.

I too was on the receiving end of the town bully, the subject of many a joke. In fact, I still remember my school bully: "Susie." (Her name has been changed in the hope she will not read this and come after me in my sleep!) Susie was an extremely aggressive girl who demanded bubble gum from me every day when I was in the sixth grade. I know what you're thinking. "Marc, a girl bullied you?" As you know, girls mature much quicker than guys, and I hadn't yet hit my growth spurt and therefore I was much smaller than "Susie". Aside from that, she was one of the toughest gals in the school, and probably one of the toughest in our town. Judge me if you must, but "Susie" was some kind of bully! I digress. I'm sure Susie turned out to be a fine, upstanding, nonthreatening citizen. In fact, if we were to interview "Susie", we'd probably find a person who herself, was a product of gross bullying.

We all have similar stories. However, I want you to understand that God can use you *because of* who you are and what you've done! I think that my provocative, joking nature as a boy has poured over into my love for people today. Although this is not a strategy per se, it is a tool God's has placed in my repertoire to help me reach people, especially the unchurched and the overlooked. I love to joke even today. God, knowing that about me, brings that influence into my interactions as well as my preaching.

We are the sum of our thoughts and experiences. God gives us a variety of experiences so we can see how frail we really are. The Psalmist suffered much loss at the hands of bad decisions only to come to the place of realizing his own frailty. David pleaded, "LORD, make me to know mine end, and the measure of my days, what it is; that I may know how frail I am." (Psalm 39:4, KJV). Notice that the Psalmist asked God to reveal this truth of his frailty, implying he was examining his *own* life once again and needed to understand his brevity.

After my father's death, following an eight-month fight with cancer, I too began to see my own frailty in light of eternity. We have but a moment to redeem our time to lead as many people to Jesus as possible. Use what you have and who you are to reach the world!

The truth is, people who poke fun, pick at, or put others down are likely unhappy with their own life. When you realize who you are in Christ, those of you who are saved will sense a sweeter spirit, a fuller peace, igniting your passion for *all* people—and you might even begin to like the person in the mirror. That kinder disposition, which is unleashed by knowing you are chosen by the Creator of the world, is the light that draws people to Jesus! This is the goal of *looking at yourself.* Be bold enough to pray, "God, search me, know me, reveal to me who I am to You, and lead me in Your way everlasting. Amen."

Yes, I am a preacher! I am a minister of the Gospel of Jesus Christ! Perhaps the reason God uses me to reach others is that I *have* messed up. Or maybe He uses me because I see how far He can bring someone through the messiness of this world, through the gate of lostness.

In fact, I began to really hear God's voice during one of the lowest points of my life. Let me lay it out in a timeline:

- In 1989 at twenty years of age, I was married.
- In 1990, we had a son. Later that year, I was deployed for Desert Storm.
- When I returned from my deployment, we built our first home.
- In 1993, my precious daughter was born.

If you are married and have experienced any of the above list, you are probably having shortness of breath about right now. Any one of these issues can cause great distress in a marriage, and like many young couples, life hit us right between the eyes. After a few normal years (whatever that looks like), we meshed right in with the rest of society. We were raising a family, barely getting by, going to church, and so on.

Then, after ten years of marriage, in 1999, I hit the low point. The inevitable happened. My dear wife, two kids, and I were becoming a statistic. Our home, our family, and our marriage was destroyed.

Without sharing all the gory details of why marriages fail—and there are thousands—I will say that I had made my fair share of reckless mistakes! Stephanie and I both saw life in a different light—not at all the light by which we had been saved but a light shining on the messiness of life. The outcome would be divorce—or at least we thought.

Since I cannot speak for Stephanie, I will briefly share my own heart. For me, life had dealt me the ultimate blow! Everything I thought I had control over had been stripped away from me and was forever lost. We were on the path to divorce, and there was nothing anyone could do to stop it.

Except God!

Now, before you get overly excited about all the details, remember, there will be none. In fact, my wife later said to someone, "Satan is not at all unique in his attacks. He uses the same tactics again and again. Why? Because they work! Whether it's infidelity, financial sin, or dishonesty, it's all the same story."

In fact, as a pastor, I have now counseled countless couples in times of conflict, and all the stories are alarmingly the same. That said, I submit to you that the outcomes can be similar as well. God is changeless, and therefore, what He did in my and Stephanie's marriage, He will do for anyone. God not only restored us, but He made us brand new! That is what God does best: He makes things new. Despite what seemed like irreconcilable differences, God brought us back together, breathing new love in our hearts, a love rooted in Him. After six months of the worst hurt I could have imagined, God had given us a new marriage—just ten days before our divorce proceedings. It's never too late to look up and cry out to God, "God, we are now out of the way. Have Your way in us."

As I began to look at myself, I realized that in that time of brokenness, I had learned to pray, to fast, and to discern the voice of God. In short, I became useable and bless-able. I saw myself in light of His glory and realized my filth before Him. He washed me clean, made me new, and spoke into my heart a call to preach His precious Word.

After a year or so following our reconciliation, I resigned from the military and stepped full-time into ministry. I later realized a prior nudging to which I had not responded. But this time, He had my full attention. I dropped everything to follow Him, with no chance of turning back. What if I just needed to take a real look at me before I could respond to His call? What if it took a broken marriage to slow me down long enough to take that real look at me? In the end, God healed my marriage. Stephanie and I fell in love and became best friends. My children saw the healing hand of a merciful

God. He even used our hurt and our loss to speak promise into other marriages that seemed to have no hope, just like ours.

Glory be to God!

🔒

Before I move on to the next topic, I feel I should add a sidebar to this thought. You may feel a tugging on your heart or a nudging in your spirit to reconcile a broken relationship, to make peace at home, to accept the calling to preach, to go in the field to mission, to teach a Sunday school class, to lead worship, to call a friend from your school days to apologize for a wrongdoing, or to do any number of other things for the glory of God. It is probably a good idea to deal with that nudging so that God can use it to its fullest, through you. This book will still be here when you get back. Go, follow Jesus!

🔒

In the spirit of full disclosure, as I began looking at me, I also began asking myself the same question as everyone else: "Marc, you're going to be a preacher? Really now?" When I knew for certain God was calling me, I had to run the thought over in my own mind several times before saying it aloud. But once I did say it, it felt right. It was God's plan to use someone like me to reach the world. And He wants to use you too. The great irony in God's economy is that He does not need our greatness. He only wants us, empty vessels willing to follow Him with hopeless abandon. His greatness is sufficient for anyone who accepts such a great calling in his or her life.

Each of our lives is unique, an extension of God's DNA, stamped onto our being. There is no one else in the entire world like you. God has a plan, a plan for you to take a look at yourself and the greatness that exists in you—and then reach out to Him for your next move. Likely, it will *not* be your talents God uses to reach the world; it will be your weaknesses! Jesus told the apostle Paul as he cried out three times to "remove the thorn in his flesh,"

My grace is sufficient for thee, my strength is made
perfect in your weakness. (2 Corinthians 12:9, KJV)

He allowed the great apostle's weakness to remain so Paul would
consistently rely on the strength of the Holy Spirit that resided in him.
This passage is one of the most profound in all of Scripture.
Notice what Jesus said to the Apostle: "My strength is made perfect."
The word "made," in this context, does not mean "created"; rather, it
means to come to light or to be manifested. Jesus is saying that His
strength, which is already perfect, is now manifested as perfect "in
your weakness." Paul's weakness was the thing he most wanted to
remove. Yet, Jesus informed Paul that it was that very weakness by
which His strength would become evident through Paul's life! If there
is something God has called you to do that you feel you cannot do,
you will find yourself relying on His strength rather than your own.
Isn't it funny how God has this all figured out? Will you allow God
to manifest His strength through your weaknesses? If so, you must
be willing first to look at you. If you do, will you like what you see?

I am reminded of a story I heard about twenty-five years ago,
while I was in the military. The story changed my life. Allow me to
paraphrase my recollection of the story. Around 1870, a man named
Dr. Russell Conwell was traveling through modern-day Iraq. His
loquacious camel guide had succeeded in telling more stories than
Dr. Conwell could tolerate. In his frustration, he snapped at his
guide and demanded he stop speaking. The guide turned to Dr.
Conwell and exclaimed sharply, "I have one more story, a story I
reserve for my most special clients—and you are my special client."

Hoping this was truly the man's final story, Dr. Conwell
reluctantly conceded.

"Just one more story."

Little did he know, this story would change his life forever. And
I must say, it changed mine too.

The guide proceeded with this story:

There was a wealthy Persian farmer named Ali Hafed. He had a wife and children and everything a man could ever want—or so he thought. One day, a traveling priest happened by Ali's farm, looking for a meal and a place to rest his head. The traveler told stories of explorers he'd heard about who were finding large diamond mines filled with millions of precious jewels.

The priest told Ali, "With a diamond the size of your finger, you could purchase this township, and with a handful of diamonds, you could buy the whole country! You could place your children on thrones adorned with jewels beyond your imagination."

That night, Ali Hafed went to bed a poor man, even though he was far from it! But considering the diamonds that existed elsewhere, he now considered himself to be poor.

The next day, he told his wife of his newfound dream—to sell his farm and pursue this great wealth. Despite her fearful disagreement, he sold his farm and set upon his journey. He traversed Africa, searching far and wide, and sailed to Europe, ultimately landing in Spain, near Barcelona, completely broke and utterly despondent. There, Ali Hafed stood, broken, shamed, and finding no reason to live another day. In his state of sadness, he decided to plunge himself into the ocean below the rock face from which he stood.

A few years had passed, and the priest made his way back to Ali Hafed's farm to visit with his old friend. Once he arrived, he heard of the terrible tragedy that had befallen his friend in his pursuit of great wealth. Upon entering the new owner's home, he saw a dark, shiny stone atop his mantle. The priest knew immediately what it was. He politely asked the new owner of Ali Hafed's farm where he had found this stone and if he knew what it was. The new owner said that while watering his camel in the garden, he saw this shiny stone in the waterbed of the creek. The priest responded, "This is an uncut diamond, bigger than any I've ever seen."

The new owner returned in a somewhat cavalier manner, "There are tons of those down there!"

In fact, Ali Hafed's farm later became one of the largest diamond mines in the entire world!

When the priest realized the incredible wealth that had been discovered on Ali Hafed's farm, he was mortified.

Dr. Russell Conwell asked his camel guide, "So, Ali spent all his wealth and lost his family when all the while, he had *acres of diamonds in his own backyard*?"

The takeaway for you and me is much the same. We often spend our life looking for some object, some angle, some great purpose or special something to fulfill our God-given potential. Then in the doxology of our life, we see it. It was there the whole time. God had providently situated us in our own "acres of diamonds," but we never saw its worth. They probably aren't literal stones, as in the case of Ali Hafed. However, the great wealth of being the best version of who God created you to be, while living out God's perfect will, is worth more than all the diamonds in the world. Consider the words of Solomon, the wisest man ever to live:

> A *good* name is to be chosen rather than great riches,
> Loving favour rather than silver and gold. (Proverbs 22:1, KJV)

We, like Ali Hafed, have everything we are seeking, and it's already in our possession. But maybe, like Ali, we don't know how to identify a diamond in the rough. God is not through with you yet! Everything you need is within you, through the precious Holy Spirit. Paul wrote to the Church in Colossae, "For in Him dwells the fullness of the Godhead bodily; and you are complete in Him, who is the head of all principality and power" (Colossians 2:9–10, NKJV). Now, take another look at you. You may not be where you want to be, but I'll bet you are not where you used to be. He's given you a new name, His fullness, and it's even better than if you had acres of diamonds on your own land.

(3)

GO AFTER THE UNCHURCHED?

Why don't we just go after the unsaved? The simple reason is that, at a glance, you and I cannot determine who is saved and who isn't. It is, however, easy to see who is not attending church. They are the ones outside the gate. In fact, hardly anyone will be offended by a simple "What church do you attend?" But you meet someone and break out the direct question: "Are you saved?"

You are liable to get a variety of answers:

> "Yep, sure am."
> "I think I am."
> "I hope so."

Even "It's none of your stinkin' business," or worse!

I have no problem speaking with someone about their salvation, but I often choose to begin with an open-ended query to generate conversation rather than a quick yes/no question that could cut the encounter short.

If you are ministering abroad, it can become even more precarious. You must learn what questions to ask and which ones to avoid. For example, "Are you a Christian?" can launch you into a world of unwanted discussion and debate. However, a more open-ended query may offer a treasure trove of useful information when getting to the main point of their relationship (or lack thereof) with Jesus. Remember, you may be trying to get them to attend a service or event where the Gospel will be preached. I know what you're thinking: What about leading them to the Lord right then and there? By all means, if the Holy Spirit should prompt you in that area, do it! But you must be sensitive to what He is saying and not just seeking a quick close. Remember, what is customary in your culture may be considered taboo in another. In short, make sure you know your audience, and know which questions *not* to ask.

For example, early in my ministry, I was visiting a lady around fifty years of age. Her family had gathered around her bedside since her medical problems had escalated. I have always been quick to speak to people about their salvation and would seek to lead people to Jesus any time the opportunity would present itself. However, that day, while standing among an already nervous family, I asked the lady, "If you died today, do you know where you will spend eternity?"

The very moment I finished the not-so-tactful question, I realized that was not a question appropriate for all people at all times. Her family snapped their heads towards me as if I had called her the worst name imaginable. After deflating any hope their loved one would ever recuperate (after all, I was the preacher with all the faith), I left with the realization there were many other questions I could have asked to determine this woman's relationship with Jesus.

How, then, do we identify the unchurched? In simple terms, it is an individual who is either not attending a local church or one who has not yet been reached with the Gospel message. In contrast, trying to reach the disgruntled church member who moves membership until they find a church that caters to their liking is not kingdom or church growth at all. In fact, that type of "church growth" is simply padding your numbers, and that's not what we are about. Don't get me wrong, we do want to accept those who've been hurt by another church, so they might heal and eventually end up in our church. But in my opinion, the best first step is to encourage them, if possible, to reconcile with their previous pastor or church. You might be surprised how that approach is, in fact, biblical. Furthermore, it is more helpful for them and you in the long run.

Most "church growth" and "church loss" can be likened to a revolving door through which the disgruntled churchgoers walk. Let me say it this way: if you stay in the ministry long enough, you will lose people. Be careful not to take too much credit when people join your church or if they choose to leave. You will be much better off not giving yourself that much credit. In fact, this may blow your mind, but you may *need* to lose some people. I have found that those who want to leave a church each time they disapprove of one of its decisions are better left to the Lord's discretion. Sadly, some people aren't happy unless they are unhappy, and you may need to shake the dust off your feet and let them go. The ones who remain deserve our tireless work and investment.

In fact, one of my heroes in the faith, Pastor Johnny Hunt gave me a great piece of advice, that I currently use for everyone who leaves my church. First, I always take the high road and though it hits me personally, I refuse to allow it to hurt me personally. Pastor Johnny told me to write a handwritten letter to the person thanking them for the time spent in my ministry. Secondly, wish them the best in this new season of worship at their new church. And lastly, encourage them to honor their new pastor in the same way they've honored you. At first glance this may seem a little manipulative, but it's not! It is a honest way to "release" them in a new work. This way, when you cross paths in the community, it will not be as awkward. They know you know they're gone, and they feel they have your blessing. It really helps, and God gets the glory!

To reach the world, old paradigms must be broken. And in some cases, this is possible only when old ideologies are removed. Real losses should concern us. These losses are best categorized as losses due to attrition. This is normal in most churches—bringing new people in the front door while losing existing members out the back. In fact, statistics show we may lose 33 to 35 percent of our church each year. That equates to an entire new congregation every few years!

Never allow your model of church growth to be driven only by growing your numbers. If you fall into this trap, you will find yourself no longer ministering to the ones with whom you've already reached. The result is losses due to high attrition rates, or fruitless turnover. In fact, I've spoken to several pastors who openly accept a complete membership flip every three to five years. That's a frightening proposition but surprisingly normal. And if you hang around long enough, you will pick up some of the remnants of another church's "losses." But that, my friend, is *not* the main goal. The goal is not simply to add to the church role but also to add to the Kingdom—and then make disciples. If you set out to grow your church, you will rarely get disciples, but if you invest in discipling people, you will always get *Church growth*! And by the way, you'll see your attrition losses diminish in the process. So, choose the type of outcome you wish to achieve, one where care ministry is the duty of every member, not just one person on your staff!

True church growth can be measured by new converts and new believers. When you reach into the unchurched community and harvest a new soul into the body of Christ, the church has experienced fruitful growth. Perhaps the most incredible part of this type of growth is that it is also the most contagious. For example, consider that long-pursued, unreachable uncle or that spouse who just wouldn't have anything to do with church? Then comes the much-used statement: "If only he would come to Christ, he would be an incredible asset for the kingdom!"

Why? Because when Jesus reaches into the orphaned soul and saves him, an adoption takes place! The result of such a change in identity yields not just a church member but a child of the King, a Body member who will stop at nothing less than reaching the world with the same hope given them.

I had the privilege of preaching a six-day revival to a congregation full of members who had not yet been "churched." It was one of the most refreshing times in my ministry. It was a smaller country church, with people who sincerely wanted to be the there. Most of them had been rescued by Jesus from a life of total chaos, including histories of criminality, imprisonment, and drug addiction. I had never seen so many tattoos and piercings in one place, let alone in one church! They even had security at the door, checking for knives upon entrance. If you didn't have one, they'd give you one for your own safety. Kidding! But may it shed light on just how the tough crowd was in attendance that day. I remember pulling my truck into the parking lot of what seemed like a biker bar. Motorcycles far outnumbered cars, but there was something different about these folks. They had a hunger I had not seen before, except in some of the Third World countries in which I'd preached. In short, I preached the Word; they believed what was preached. They applied what they learned, and life change occurred!

On the third day of the revival, I spoke with the pastor before the service and shared my analysis of the attendees. His response rocked me to the core spiritually. In his Mayberry country drawl, he said, "Hey, man, you tell 'em, and they'll do it. Guess they don't know no better!" I love it!

In fact, the week after I completed the revival, my wife and I drove by that country church, and the following words were on the kiosk out front: "Somebody call 911. This church is on *fire!*"

You see, the difference was that the pastor was reaching the unchurched, untouched, and unprogrammed, orphans looking for the answer to all life's questions. The thing is, when they found it in Jesus, the church got much more than a number on the membership rolls. They were birthing new members of the body of Christ, and the fruit that would ensue was undeniable.

A few years ago, I had the opportunity to see a man we'll call Allen come to Christ. He had avoided the church for many years due to the following reasons:

> hypocrites
> rules
> commitments
> changes to his lifestyle

But on the Sunday morning he attended our church, God reached into his broken heart. He let go of the past that had him bound, said goodbye to drugs and the ways of the world, and cried out to a Holy God! That day, at that very moment, all inhibitions were thrown to the wind. The result was total transformation! He was saved and propelled into a life of reaching others far from God. He became, in months, a better evangelist of the lost, the undone, and the disenfranchised than many who had been Christians for a lifetime. Why? Because he was unchurched for so long, he now saw the truth through a "time is of the essence" mindset, to tell the rest of the world what he had found! He had gone from a life of drinking and drug use to a life of daily bread, almost instantaneously! Yes, give me an unchurched crowd with whom to share the Good News. They are all-in! Today, Allen and his wife have invested in countless lives and have even invested financially in the work to reach this next generation for Jesus.

To the unchurched convert, the Gospel comes like the medicine to the world's most aggressive cancer. They want to quickly and deliberately spread this "new" medicine of healing and hope before it's too late for others who are sin-sick, just like they were.

According to the *World Population Review*, approximately 163,898 people die every day around the world. If nearly one-sixth the world's population has never heard the Gospel, then around 27,316 people die every day having *never heard* the message of Jesus Christ! This is why the unchurched must hear about the love and redemption offered us by Jesus! That is why the RUSH strategy exists. Identify the unchurched and become invested in that community of people. This is where most local churches fall short of the great commission. Scripture assures us, "The harvest truly is plentiful, but the laborers are few"(Matthew 9:37, NKJV). Overseas missions, disaster relief, and so on are sometimes the mold for missions. The problem is we can't forget the local mission: the unchurched in your own backyard! And let's not forget the latter part of this commission: "The laborers are few." What was true when Jesus spoke those words still reigns supreme today. The majority of the church does not wish to "work" or "labor" to reach those on the outside. You see, that type of personal evangelism costs you something, hence the word "laborers." That's why we resort to a "build it and they'll come" type of ideology rather than a "work force" that will do what it takes to reach the lost. Laboring speaks of effort, and effort speaks of personal exertion, and exertion costs. I think the church has become ideologically lazy, and no one really wants to "go," or feel responsible for the lost. However, if I may use the mantra of my Atlanta Falcons, it's time to "Rise up!" It's time to stand up and be counted, to join the ranks of those men and women who've gone before us in reaching the lost. After all, someone came *through the gate* for you!

God, help us to take our place, to go after the unchurched. Through them, we can reach the world!

4

MEET THEM WHERE THEY ARE!

So now that we know the unchurched, how do we reach them? How do we get them to attend our church? The simple answer is you invite them! As I search through all the "church growth principles" and "how to reach people" manuals, one thing I can say with full certainty: you will never reach the unchurched if you don't engage them in some way! It seems a little too simple. Well, there is more.

I think we have all heard the statement, "If you want to reach someone, you must meet them where they are!" I too believe that. However, when I do that, I quickly move from meeting them where they are, to bringing them to where I am. This typical "reaching people" philosophy can actually push more people away from church than it will ever bring them in. The simple reason is usually our methods to reach people are feeble attempts to change them, before they are ready to be members of the body of Christ. Unfortunately, as many a well-intended spouse can attest, you cannot change anyone, so rather than making the effort to bring someone around to your way of thinking, just meet them in their element. Meet them where, and as they are.

The main point of this strategy is to understand your role in the reaching process. Remember when Jesus called the fisherman by the Sea of Galilee? He said to them, "follow me," which is to say, "Come to where I am," "and I will make you fishers of men," which is to say, "Go where they are." First of all, only Jesus can "call" a man from where He is, as is evident when He "calls" these men to become His disciples. But notice what he then says, "I will make You 'fishers' of men." (Matthew 4:19, KJV) He did not call you and me to be the bait, and certainly, He did call you to be the cleaners of the fish—just fisherman. You see, as we try to reach people, we do so by trying to make them look, sing, think, respond, and worship like we do. That may be why so many churches are full of the same kind of people. You will notice, despite the many efforts to reach a multicultural audience, most churches are still all white, all Hispanic, all Korean, all black, and so on. And in most churches everyone wears suits or everyone wears jeans. For the most part, the people sitting next to you in church are just like you.

Where are all the lost people? Most churches are full of self-proclaimed believers who attend church every week while never once inviting a lost person to the service. Why is that? The problem is evident. And let me warn you: this may sting a little. We are either too busy or just lack the passion for the lost, especially if they look different than we do. We are all different, and therefore, the outflow of our worship can be completely different one from another too. So rather than trying to alter the certainty of our differences, we should use that diversity to the Kingdom's advantage, and in so doing, we become more appealing to the lost.

Look at it this way: we spend a lot of time trying to make people look a certain way, when all we really need to do is point them to the One who can change them from the inside out. As one discipling another, helping a new convert to understand biblical doctrine, which brings about a subsequent change, is very important. But make sure you are speaking of Biblical doctrine and not just your church doctrine or even a denominational dogma, which can push people away. That is, you are trying to bring them to your way of thinking. And once again, that is not the goal. Once they are redeemed, we disciple them in a proper walk with the Lord, according to biblical precepts, and true change will occur.

But long before a new convert can or is even willing to comprehend doctrine, he or she must first see God's love, a love that has no bounds, a love that meets them right where they are, a love that surrounds their hurting soul and draws them in their vulnerability and introduces them to Jesus. You see, it is only because of the love of Jesus that we can be alive in Him. It is that "love [that] covers a multitude of sin"(1 Peter 4:8, NLT) When you share how Jesus, who is fully God, left His perfect throne in heaven to, dwell among us" (John 1:1,14, KJV), to seek after us, even the toughest, most hardened criminal will be all ears. Share Jesus and the cross, but do so in the manner in which God intended, as a "free gift" (Romans 6:23, KJV), not a prerequisite to be like you or some exclusive social club, as they see it.

To state the obvious, Jesus's earthly ministry model was the best example of the kind of witnessing we should strive to emulate. He had a demonstrative way of meeting people right where they were, speaking their *language* even if in the lowest of circumstances. When Jesus went into a fishing community, he spoke of them becoming "fishers of men." When He went into a farming community, He spoke of sowing and reaping, seedtime/harvest, and threshing floors. He even reached people in the scum-ridden slums of the world, such as lepers, prostitutes, and, even worse, Auburn fans and IRS agents. (Sorry, I couldn't resist, and all the DAWG fans said, "Amen!")

Though Jesus never condoned peoples' illicit behavior, He somehow had a way of walking into their world and loving them to His own. Consider some specific situations in your life where you've tried to reach people where they were. How did you do? Did you succeed? If not, why? Did you take Jesus to where they were, or did you try to bring them to where your presumptions of Jesus lie? You may only get one shot to point someone to Jesus. Be ready to make it count! Spend less effort convincing someone how wonderful it is to be a child of the Most High and more time loving them in their current state so they crave the love you currently experience in Christ. The Holy Spirit will begin to woo them from where there are to where God is waiting with open arms. This may sound like a sort of *easy believe-ism*, but it's not that at all! I just think too many of us put the cart before the horse, expecting people to live a holy life long before they have even met the Holy One. Show them Jesus in your life, and they will begin to hunger after the righteousness of Jesus they see in you!

I have to constantly remind myself what I must have looked like before someone shared Jesus's love with me. I was a mess. I was indifferent. I was cynical. I was in unbelief. And so were you! You and I were just the orphans outside the gate—hopeless, nameless, and lost. Never forget that someone reached through the gate for you.

Now, if you're like me, as you survey your past attempts to share Jesus, you may feel like a complete and utter failure. But you need to realize, you are not Jesus! I know, I know, but Marc we have the same Spirit, the Holy Spirit, living in us. Sure! But Jesus relinquished self, presuppositions, ideologies, and fully released Himself into the Spirit of God, to perfection! Our humanity more often limits us in the area of full surrender, regardless of how hard we try. Our efforts are feeble and foolish at best. Remember, Jesus said on many occasions that He had come "not to do my own will, but the will of Him who sent me" (John 6:38, NKJV). If we could trust God with that same mindset, a more successful evangelism paradigm would ensue, and fruit would come!

But again, since we are human and therefore bring flesh to the process, we will likely make mistakes. So, what then? Should we just give up on the lost if they do not look like, talk like, or act like us? No way! We must, however, move self out of the way and operate as best we can in the Spirit, like Jesus did!

For example, in His humanity, Jesus would not have connected with non-Jews. It was contrary to culture and law. It would have been against the grain of everything He was as a Jew. But since He was in total surrender to His Father's will, he looked beyond the vast differences, the cultural expectancy, and the law and loved even gentiles with the same relentless pursuit! That's what He wants from you and me—to love those in which we have nothing else in common. Can you do that? Or do you build a wall between you and those who are much different than you?

Jesus said it this way: "If anyone desires to come after Me, let him deny himself, and take up his cross daily, and follow Me." (Luke 9:23, KJV). Remember you were one choice away from being right where they are before your encounter with King Jesus. You might have even been worse! You are not right with God today because you were any more approachable, teachable, loveable, or reachable. You are a child of God today because of a loving God and perhaps a servant who was willing to share Jesus with you—right where you were. To get them to where you are now, redeemed, you must meet them where they are, undone and hopeless.

The idea of this strategy can be summed up in a word: love. Do you really love God's people? That's the real big question. Do you care that people all around you may be on their way to hell? Don't allow the proposition of hell for some to escape your mind as you navigate the thoughts of personal evangelism. Scripture states, "By this shall all men know that ye are my disciples, if ye have love one to another" (John 13:35, KJV). Jesus asked Peter a simple yet profound question after the three-time denial and cursing of His Lord. Jesus said, "Peter, do you love me?"

To which Peter responded on the third time, "Of course I do Lord."

Ironically, this was the same thing Peter said before He denied his Jesus the night He was arrested in the garden. Jesus did not recite some long parable or exhortation. No. Jesus looked Peter square in the face and said, "Feed my sheep" (John 21:17, KJV). I love this language since the Shepherd-sheep relationship was unique, to say the least, and we as sheep, are to be fruitful in making or bearing more sheep who, like us, depend fully on the Good Shepherd, Jesus!

You see, both the writers and the audience fully understood

the shepherd-sheep relationship Jesus spoke about. The shepherd would leave the comforts of his home and take up residency in the field with his sheep. But he didn't stop there. The shepherd would eat, sleep, and live with his sheep for an extended period. He would be the provider, companion, and protector of his sheep at all costs. The "Good Shepherd gives His life for His sheep" (John 10:11, NKJV). It was a given for the Shepherd to risk his own life for that of his sheep. That is why Psalm 23 is so insightful in its application. The language is beautiful: "The Lord is my Shepherd; I shall not want" (Psalm 23:1, KJV). The most powerful pronouns that stand out in this text are "my" and "I." When we personalize Psalm 23 in our own walk with Jesus, we enter into greatest shepherd-sheep relationship—that of the Chief Shepherd and us, the un-insightful sheep. I think it is fair to assume, the shepherd met the sheep where they were! And so should we.

In times of antiquity, the religious crowd of the day, the Pharisees, saw themselves as the gatekeepers of the law and of righteousness. They saw everyone else as less than. In their minds, the ones to whom they ministered or represented were mindless sheep. Yet, they operated in stark contrast to the Good Shepherd. One of the greatest tools we can use as gatekeepers to the Good News of Jesus is to be reminded of the "open door" Jesus "set before" the Church of Philadelphia, which is the true church (Revelation 3:7–8, KJV). Meeting people outside the gate works best when the gate is not locked but open wide!

Let me give you a recent example of "meeting people where they are." I was invited to speak at a church in Toronto, Ontario. I made this trip with my wife, who ministered in song prior to my preaching. Now, let me say that before I travel, I check and double-check to make sure I have my essentials (i.e., suit, tie, shoes, iPhone, iPad, MacBook Air, sermon, etc.), you know, the essentials. I did not, however, check my wife's baggage to ensure that she had all her essentials. In fact, that could be a frightening proposition, since her essentials are much more vast in number and much more essential than mine! I consider it is far above a husband's paygrade to inspect such a precious cargo. As fate would have it, the next day, we were in our hotel room getting dressed, and my wife realized she had forgotten to bring her hairbrush, one of her essentials! If you're a woman reading this, you know how big of a deal this is! If you're a man reading this and you don't realize how important this is, consider yourself informed. Like any good husband worth his weight, I had received and acknowledged my mission. I got dressed and proceeded to the lobby to find a brush. After realizing the hotel didn't make it easy for a brother, and not willing to fail at this important mission, I put plan B into effect: Who could give me a ride? I noticed a gentleman standing rather inconspicuously in a corner of the room. After a short introduction, I convinced this airport shuttle driver into giving me a ride down the street to a drug store. My wife says I never meet a stranger, for which I am very thankful, especially in that moment.

Now, to the spiritual lesson. As the driver and I began the short trip to the store, God began speaking to my heart about this man setting just inches away from me. After a few small exchanges in conversation, I realized *why* my wife left her brush at home. God had ordained this moment, for this time, for the sole purpose of this man! I knew God was up to something big when a man clearly from another part of the world had the same name as me. Marc told me that he was from Sri Lanka and had travelled to the United States eighteen years earlier for emergency surgery. While he was in the States, he got news his entire family had been killed during the civil war that was ongoing in his country. This gentleman had escaped death by just days. After hearing the news that his family was dead, he sought political asylum in Canada and later became a Canadian citizen. Go, Canada!

This gentleman was born into a Roman Catholic family but later converted to Buddhism. After a few questions about his faith, I realized he was not saved and God had sent me all the way to Canada to share the Hope of the world with this man. Rather than trying to speak to him in theological terms or debate religion, I just *met him where he was*, a man who had suffered great loss and one desperately needing a savior. He needed Jesus and didn't even know it, but I did. Although my next words were very direct, the Holy Spirit nudged me. I looked him in the eyes and asked him if he'd ever thought of the afterlife, in light of eternity. The Spirit further nudged. As he shook his head yes, acknowledging his thoughts of eternity, I asked if he knew where he would spend eternity had he too had died in the Civil War that had taken his family. A tear slowly ran down his cheek, and then another. His body language invited more, as if he stood with his face pressed through a locked gate, just like the orphans had years before. I shared some of my own inhibitions concerning religion, which cannot save anyone, and told him of my relationship with Jesus Christ, who can save *everyone*. As this precious man learned of the sacrificial love of my Jesus on the cross and how He came to redeem us all, he was all ears. As the car's heater fan noised in the background, his heart was receptive for an encounter with King Jesus.

The Greek word for redeemed is *exagorazo*, which means to be bought from the slave market, rescued (*Strong's Concordance Greek*, 1805). As he learned that Jesus paid for his life with his own, he was awestruck. Some of his childhood learnings in the Old Testament came resounding back into his memory. He remembered the story of the sacrificial lamb which covered the Israelites sins on the Day of Atonement (Leviticus 16:8–34, KJV). He recalled how God remembered Noah and gave him a way out of the flood (Genesis 8:1, KJV). He spoke of how Abram told Isaac, "God will provide Himself a lamb for the burnt offering" (Genesis 22:8, KJV) and on and on! You could see it is his eyes; he knew what I was telling him was true, and he wanted more! He said, "I never put two and two together; Jesus was that lamb right! He died once and for all, even for me, and the ark, the sacrificial lamb. All was pointing to Jesus, who made a way out for all men, even me!"

I called him by his name: "Marc, Do you want to be rescued?

Do you want to know the kind of love only Jesus can give you? Will you allow the Lamb of God, Jesus Christ, to take away your sin?"

He reached for my hand and said while smiling like a little child on Christmas morning. "I *do* want this. I want to have that love in my heart."

Right there, in a car in front of Walgreens, Jesus *met him right where he was,* both physically and spiritually. He prayed and asked Jesus Christ into his heart! I had just reached an unchurched man who was hopelessly lost with a simple dialogue, speaking of a profound truth. I too had met him where he was—a dead man in need of a life-giving Savior. All I did was in obedience, tell him of Jesus, and the Holy Spirit did the rest. God had reached another *through the gate.* Go, God!

That encounter with the bus driver is not the only time this has happened to me. I believe God uses things like a forgotten brush to place you into peoples' lives in that very moment, for a specific purpose. Don't miss it! Don't complicate it! Just meet them where they are!

Perhaps even more telling of this principle is the story of a sweet dear friend of mine, Elissa Williams. While serving in a local church as pastor to students, I got a dreadful call one summer day in 2007. This day was like any other—at least that's what I thought until I received a call from one of my student's mother. When I answered, her voice was frantic. She asked me to meet her at the hospital, her two-year-old nephew had fallen in the pool.

I dropped what I was doing and sped off to the hospital. I had performed this same routine on several occasions, but this time was different. I just didn't realize how this moment would change my life. When I arrived, I found the family in the waiting room reserved for people with exceptional medical cases, usually a life-threatening situation. The moment I entered the room, I knew things were grave. The mother of this little child lay prostrate on the cold, dirty, floor crying out to God for her baby boy. Her precious son, Caden, was fighting for his life in another room. At this moment, all this mother wanted or needed in life was for her little angel to pull through. I soon realized the gravity of the situation and that Caden had actually drowned.

In that moment, you don't offer solutions. You don't quote Scripture. Not to sound heretical, but the Scripture in Romans 8:28 (KJV), "all things work together for good," just won't do in a moment like that. I got down on the floor with her, reached for her hands, and cried out to God with her! In that moment, I met her where she was, a parent in need of a miracle. You see, I too was a parent. In my fervency of prayer, I experienced an empathy I had not previously known. I prayed like I had never prayed before. I prayed as if Caden was my son. After what seemed like hours of effectual prayer, the doctor entered the room. All eyes were fixed on him.

"I'm sorry, we did all we could do," the doctor almost shamefully admitted. Two-year-old Cade had died.

In the days, months, and even years to come, I tried to wrap my head around what had transpired on that dreadful day. How could God use this for any good? Had I failed in that moment? I didn't feel I had offered any solace for that broken family. Could there even be any solace in such a brokenness? I was at a loss. And though God is not obligated to answer all our questions, He finally answered that question for me seven years later.

I kept in touch with Elissa over the years. But one day, as I was studying for a sermon series, God impressed me to call her and invite her to assist me with a very special sermon at the new church in which I was serving. I planned to interview different people who had been through tough situations in hopes of answering the tough questions we all might ask. I asked how the death of a child could possibly work into God's will and work any good in the life of another? Elissa told us of her battles and the near loss of her marriage due to Cade's death. She further spoke of their reconciliation and a new calling on her life to minister to troubled women. While given a devotion to several women in a shelter one day, Elisa met eyes with a lady who happened to be a devout Muslim. She recalls this lady rolling her eyes as the Scriptures were read aloud. The Holy Spirit spoke to Elisa, nudging her to share her testimony about her Cade. Reluctant to do so because of the tremendous pain she would be forced to relive, Elisa faithfully conceded. She told her most painful story of the loss of her precious Cade.

As Elisa spoke of Cade's death, and more importantly, God's grace *in* Cade's death, this Muslim lady perked up as if she struck a chord. This woman also had a son, who at the time was six years old. After the meeting, she told Elisa she wanted to know more about this Jesus, who had gotten her through such a tragedy. God was at work in ways Elissa could not have known at the time. You see, as we are "meeting people where they are," the Holy Spirit is also meeting and drawing them. Elisa shared the precious gospel with her, and in that moment, she trusted Jesus as her Lord! Could it be possible? Had God actually used two-year-old Cade's death to open a door, thus leading this precious lady to Jesus?

This is a good place to insert Romans 8:28 and shout, "Hallelujah!" Something good had *actually* come out of Cade's seemingly senseless death. Elissa was beginning to see that in Cade's death, lives were now being impacted. What a legacy little Cade would have in the lives of so many! But as the old sindicated radio personality, Paul Harvey would say, "And now, the rest of the story."

In just one short year following the eternal transformation of this mother, Elissa got the most disturbing phone call of her life. The seven-year-old son of the Muslim lady Elissa had led to Jesus had drowned in a pool, in much the same way as Cade. Elissa had suffered a loss most of us pray we will never comprehend. She hurt. She struggled. She nearly died from the pain of losing her precious son Cade. Years later, God called Elissa to teach a Bible study, but rather than just teaching some prepackaged, one-size-fits-all message, Elissa just met them where they were, broken and undone. This once-lost Muslim lady had been eternally redeemed and furthermore, her precious son who died just one year later, and today, He is in the precious arms of Jesus—and, oh yeah, he's hanging out with Cade!

5

KEEP IT SIMPLE

Perhaps one of the quickest ways to discourage the unchurched is to complicate the simplicity of the Gospel of Jesus Christ. Simplicity seems a bit oxymoronic since God is so infinitely complex, right? Well, it may seem that way, but it's not. God expects us to keep the main thing, the main thing. The complexity actually comes in when our finite minds try to "explain" something an infinite God meant to be simple. He reminds us of the simplicity of His Word. Paul asserted in 2 Corinthians 11:3 (NKJV), "But I fear, lest somehow, as the serpent deceived Eve by his craftiness, so your minds may be corrupted from the simplicity that is in Christ."

Why on earth do we as preachers, students, teachers, and laypeople insist on complicating coming to Jesus? The quick answer is someone probably made it complicated when it was presented to us. God, help us to leave the complexities out of the gospel. Jesus died for all "for God so loved ... whosoever will, let him come," and so on. That's simple enough, isn't it? Throw the intricate "plan of salvation" aside and just introduce them to the "Man of salvation," Jesus. It's meant to be simple.

In my more recent studies of Scripture, specifically as it pertains to leadership or pastoring, I have been forced to reckon with the paradox of certain biblical teachings, which may bring us to much complexity. For example, you want to be first. The Bible teaches us to be last (Matthew 20:16, KJV). You want to be great? The Bible teaches us to become less (James 4:10, KJV). And my favorite: you want to really challenge and confound the wise? Then use the foolishness of preaching His word to do so (1 Corinthians 1:27, KJV). Therein lies the paradoxical simplicity of God's Word!

In our world, such teachings are counterintuitive, but in God's economy, they're fundamental. Think about it this way: the Psalmist says in Psalm 24:1 (KJV), "The earth is the LORD's, and all its fullness, The world and those who dwell therein." And in 2 Corinthians 8:9 (NKJV), Paul says, "Yet for your sakes He became poor, that you through His poverty might become rich." Is that simple enough for you?

The other thing (and I really hate to admit this as a pastor): according to Evantell.org, more than 95 percent of the church does not know how to lead someone to Jesus (http://www.evantell.org/ EvangelismTraining.aspx). If that statistic is true, most of you will tremble at my next question, so take a second to prepare yourself mentally and spiritually for this one. Have *you* led someone to Christ this week? What about this month? Okay, then, what about ever? Most studies reveal the same: the majority of evangelical Christians have *never* personally led anyone to Jesus! And perhaps more telling, they don't know *how* to lead someone to the Lord. If that is you, I challenge you to ask God to guide you into such an encounter this week. And remember to keep it simple.

Here's simple. Jesus Christ was God in the flesh (John 1:1,14, KJV). He left heaven, came to earth, and paid the debt we owed for our sin (Romans 6:23a, KJV). And before you even consider your own righteousness, remember that you, me, and anyone else who has ever taken a breath of air has "sinned and fallen short of such glory" (Romans 3:23, KJV). But God, deciding before time began, answered the dilemma of our disobedience with His love and grace (unmerited favor) to give us the glorious gift of eternal life (Romans 6:23b, KJV). That's how you may be made right with God. You must simply believe, confess, and repent of your sin (that is, to admit it and turn away from it), ask for forgiveness, and invite Jesus into your heart to save you, and "thou shall be saved" (Romans 10:, 9 KJV). Keep in mind, there is no magical prayer, magical words, or plan of salvation that will transform your life. It is not just believing, saying a few words, or joining a church that can save the lost. Paul says in Ephesians 2:8–9 (NKJV) that "it is by grace through faith that we are saved ... not of yourselves, lest you boast."

It is believing, trusting, repenting, and receiving, all rolled up into a real, personal relationship with Jesus Christ! Simply put, when you are forgiven and redeemed, there will be definitive life change. You will look, act, and become different.

Are you serious? Can it be so simple? To this, I respond: it must be, or else it would not be called a "gift" (Romans 6:12b, KJV). I know some of you reading this might be skeptical of such simplicity. I was too, until I met Jesus. It's through His love we can receive such a gift. But we must understand the complexities of redemption from His perspective. For example, what is offered as free to us costs Him everything! So, if it helps you, it was not free or simple for Jesus. But because He took the complexities upon Himself, it became simple for you and me. It's not a prayer. It's not the shaking of a preacher's hand at the end of a service. It is not a baptism in a pool of water. It is not having your name on some church role. **In fact, and I say this without apology, you can say a thousand prayers, be dunked in dozens of baptisteries, and have your name on every church role in town and still miss Jesus completely!** It is a simple, unadulterated, unapologetic, receiving of the finished work He has completed on the cross. And for the self-critic who feels unworthy to receive such a gift, you are in good company. We all should feel unworthy. But by grace, we can be made right. Second Corinthians 5:21 (KJV) reads, "For he hath made Him [Jesus] to be sin for us, who knew no sin; that we might be made the righteousness of God in Him." Simply, it is all about Jesus and what He did and very little about you, anyway.

In addition to being made right, there's the personal relationship with Jesus. You see, what starts with a prayer of faith is tempered through His marvelous grace, and it is effectuated in a real lifelong relationship!

A good illustration of this is the relationship I have with my wife, Stephanie. Before we were married, I wanted to be in a relationship with her, my future bride, so I pursued her (even though I always tell people she pursued me). I began to woo her into wanting a lifelong relationship with me. Then, three and a half years later, I humbled myself to the point of a taking knee, I presented her with a ring, and gently asked for her hand in marriage.

She replied, "Heck yeah, you good-looking hunk of man!" (Sorry, I got carried away. She just said "yes.") This is where the story moves from simple to complex.

Let's say she had said, "Wait" or "Maybe" or "Let me think about it." What if she had said, "No"? Then, despite my love for her and my willingness for lifelong commitment, the marriage would not have happened, at least until she accepted the offer to be my wife. But since she said, "Yes," we entered into a marriage covenant and she changed her name and became a Pritchett, my precious bride. And despite the many hardships and close encounters with our demise, thirty-one years later, she's still my beautiful bride! In fact, *because* of the ups and downs, she's more beautiful today than the day we met in the summer of 1986!

Salvation is not much different. Jesus is the groom, you and I are his betrothed bride, relentlessly pursued by Him. Jesus, through the Holy Spirit, woos us into considering a lifelong relationship. And when we are primed for the question, He speaks: "I died for you, and I now live so you too may live eternally with me." With the most gentle, perfect, inviting, and loving whisper, He pops the question: "Will you be mine? Will you enter this lifelong, and eternal relationship with me? Will you allow me to love you with a perfect love that casts out all fear? I will never leave or forsake you. Today, will you marry me?"

Then the choice is then yours. If you say, "Yes," your name is changed to His, your position is changed to forgiven, and instead of a ring, He gives you a white robe of righteousness ("He who knew no sin"). And the coolest part is the relationship is forever! And despite what our culture teaches, this marriage will not end in divorce. And if we add to or take away from that simplicity, we might as well tell Jesus, "Not right now " or "Let me think about it." In short, when we complicate it, we miss it.

Keeping it simple is paramount when reaching through the gate. The unchurched outside the gate are not clued-in to all the religious jargon. Don't preach yourself out of bringing someone to Christ by luring them into church tradition or insisting they dress a certain way or whatever else we think they have to do to be *right* with God. Just show them Jesus!

I have been privy to literally see thousands of people come to Jesus by simple means. Over 18,000 in our ministry alone! And to all the skeptics in the crowd who say, "Marc, do you really think they all got saved?"

First of all, why even go there in the first place? But since some will ask this question, yes, I am naive enough to think that *anyone* can be saved by simply asking Jesus into their heart, by saying yes to the marriage offer Jesus made to us all on the cross. I do, however, believe this is the beginning for the new convert. After all, the Bible mentions the word "Christian" only two times and "disciple" more than 270 times in the Kings James Bible. Where do you think we should place emphasis? Reach them, and then disciple them into a personal walk with Jesus. The evidence of that relationship will be seen in production of fruit—the fruit of the Spirit, "love, joy, peace, longsuffering, kindness, goodness, faithfulness, gentleness, self-control" (Galatians 5:22–23, NKJV). After all, spiritual fruit is the truest litmus test for the new convert. Simply, are you producing fruit?

Not only is coming to Jesus a simple process but remaining with Him should also be simple. I recently ministered to a childhood friend, Kevin, who had become very ill and was hospitalized. After we spoke for a few moments, the Holy Spirit began to impress upon me to make certain of his relationship with the Lord. Kevin told me he had been saved when he was younger, but after a very rough life, he was no longer saved today. He further added, "I have been so angry with God, even to the point of telling him I no longer believed in Him." Kevin thought since things had gotten so bad and his depression and bitterness had ruled his life for so long, he was no longer a child of God.

Before I qualify this point with simplicity, I encourage you not to over-spiritualize this point but rather to see it at its rudimentary and simple, face value. I proceeded to speak with Kevin about his two sons. The dialogue went something like this:

Me: Do you love your sons?

Kevin: More than any other thing in this world!

Me: Have they ever failed you?

Kevin: Yes, but not nearly as much as I have failed them.

Me: But, Kevin, when they failed you, cursed you because you failed them, or maybe even said they no longer wanted you to be their dad, would they cease being your sons?

Kevin: No! Nothing could change my love for my children. They will always be my sons.

Me: So, Kevin, let me get this straight. You're telling me that you, an imperfect man with self-admitted flaws at every turn, who can't keep things together, can *still* love your sons and continue to be their father even if they told you they hated you? But the Creator of the universe, lover of your soul, pursuer of the wretched, redeemer of mankind, Great Physician to the sick; the perfect, sinless lamb of God; cannot still love you and be your Father because of your failures? Seriously?

Kevin: [with tears streaming down his face] I guess He can. [With a big, deep breath] So I *am* still a child of God? Sounds too simple.

Me: Yes, sir, Kevin, you are! And yes, sir, it is *that* simple! Now, let's talk repentance and a restored fellowship with the Master.

And though we are still God's children, vast are the ramifications of our sin and the effects of living outside the perfect will of God. Consider Kevin. What's the potential for his cursing God and living consistently out of God's will? About four months from that encounter, Kevin died from a sudden, massive Heart attack.

So, Marc, are you saying that's what we get if we disobey God—death? I am not saying that at all, but I am saying that when God adopted you, He settled your eternity forever. You were not made right based on your righteousness or being good enough. You were redeemed and made right with God by His finished work on the cross and His glorious resurrection. But I do submit this sentiment. If you live outside His protection and favor, you could be setting yourself up for a destructive life or perhaps even a premature death. The years of heavy drinking, leading to depression and subsequent liver problems, took Kevin's life. But all that was a byproduct of his sin. In addition, Kevin will miss some great fellowship with his precious sons and their children. Sin has its costs, but to keep it simple, Jesus paid it all, and once you are His, you are His forever.

The unchurched, the spiritual orphans outside the gate, need you and me to tell them the truth, plain and simple. I love James's final words at the close of the Jerusalem Council, as the religious Jews were trying to complicate the message of hope found through a relationship with Jesus: "And so my judgment is that we should not make it difficult for the Gentiles who are turning to God (Acts

NLT). Did you get that? How about I flip that one around and rephrase it in my own words: "Let's keep being saved simple and not complicate it for those *outside the gate*." And once we have reached them with the truth, it is time to disciple them into a personal relationship with Jesus. And, oh yeah, keep that simple too!

6

USE YOUR FAILURES

As I stated in the introduction, God will use you not only in spite of your mishaps, but because of them. In part, the reason is God uses people who have often risked everything to gain hope, happiness, and meaning. Think about it this way. Jesus used some pretty tough characters to tell the great story of His redemption plan. In fact, He entered into partnership with these questionable men to effectuate His earthly ministry. Consider Peter, a man whose resume would not make it through the first round of most pulpit committees' fine-toothed comb. Peter, in his impetuous manner, would have told a couple of pulpit committees to "get a life." I mean, come on, this dude was a fisherman, perhaps even a lying potty mouth. (Have you ever known a fisherman who didn't curse and tell a tall tale?) And if that weren't enough, he even denied being a follower of Christ and cursed the Savior, his best friend of three and a half years.

Talk about failures! But God in His sovereignty, mercy, and grace, used Peter *because of* his many shortcomings. He knew what Peter could become with the right formula. And He was right! Ironically, we in the church, the religious crowd, are quick to throw someone like Peter to the curb. God, on the other hand, uses them despite their mishaps.

After Peter's encounter with the resurrected Jesus, this cursing, lying, failure of a man would be an integral part of thousands being saved and would lead the Church after Pentecost. Why? I've asked the same question a thousand times. Simply put, I have no idea why God would use that kind of person to do such great things, but that's why I wasn't chosen to redeem the world. Jesus was! Perhaps the greatest evidence of God's love is seen in the lives of those who have royally failed Him. Now before you flag down a ride on the "so we must sow my wild oats and get a testimony" bandwagon, I am not saying you *must* fail to be used of God. I *am* saying God can use you even when you do!

I am propelled to a place of such awe every time I read how Peter denied Jesus, then subsequently led thousands to Him. In fact, he even got to the point of closeness with God, people were bringing their sick into the streets so Peter's shadow could be cast on them and be healed!

> As a result of the apostles' work, sick people were brought out into the streets on beds and mats so that Peter's shadow might fall across some of them as he went by(Acts NLT)

Now, that's what I call turning over a new leaf! In fact, it's been noted by traditional scholars, such as Clement of Rome (about AD 90), Ignatius (about AD 110), and Tertullian (about AD 195), that Peter died in Rome, by crucifixion, during the persecution of Nero in AD 64. Some historians even attest, Peter was actually brought out to be crucified on a cross as Jesus had been, he refused stating his unworthiness to die like his Savior, so he was crucified upside down—at his own request. Whether he died upright or chose the latter to make his final statement of humility and honor for Jesus, his martyrdom is certain. I still find it quite fascinating that Jesus would use such a guy to proclaim this new message of salvation unto all. But again, Jesus sees what we can be and not as we even see ourselves in the present.

Consider Saul of Tarsus, the man responsible for many Christian deaths, to include, Stephen, the first Christian martyr (Acts 7:58, KJV). Saul made it his purpose in life to destroy anyone who followed Jesus of Nazareth. Yet, this same Jesus chose to meet him on a road to Damascus as he travelled to kill even more Christians. This unlikely encounter would forever transform his life into the apostle Paul. This man had, by all accounts, failed in the highest degree, yet God used him to plant churches, lead missionary journeys, and go on to write nearly two-thirds of the New Testament! Why? Because God uses our messy failures to tell of His glorious love.

Not convinced? Consider four of the five women mentioned in the lineage of Jesus in Matthew's gospel account. I preached a message once entitled "The 'Mess' in Messiah," from Matthew's Gospel (KJV), outlining these women. In chapter 1, we read of the following women, and I've taken the liberty to annotate their messiness.

How's this for messy? Only one of these five was a chaste virgin, an honorable woman, Mary, a descendant of the chosen race. From her womb, the Christ child was directly born (v. 16). Among the remaining women are Tamar, Rahab, Ruth (v. 5), and Bathsheba, who had been the wife of Uriah (v. 6). Some were Gentiles, some were remarried, and three were ever sinful. Tamar committed incest (Genesis 38:6–30, KJV); Rahab was a prostitute (Joshua 2:1, KJV); the origin of Ruth was incest, for she belonged to the tribe of Moab (Ruth 1:4, KJV), the fruit of Lot's incestuous union with his daughter (Genesis 19:30–38, KJV); and Bathsheba committed adultery with King David, which later resulted in the death of their son and her husband (2 Samuel 11;12:1–19, KJV).

Through these women, God reveals His sovereign will as it pertains to our utter failures as a sinful people. What an evil! If you're like me, you don't look so bad when placed in a lineup with the likes of Saul, Peter, and some of these women. But in truth,

---

you and I are about the same as these. We have denied Him—or at least His power, love, mercy, and grace. We have cursed Him—or at least His matchless name, which was too Holy to even utter in times of antiquity. We have even persecuted His followers through our jealousy and pride! Yet, even with my failures, Jesus called me to preach His wonder and renown.

You see, we should be nothing short of amazed by His love and forgiveness. After all, we know how bad we've been. We see our filth. And once we understand and embrace (even in the slightest), His love for us, and His forgiveness, we will inevitably begin our pursuit to lead others to Him. It becomes our natural response.

This is extremely important to understand because almost every time I speak to a nonbeliever, I hear the same thing: "How could Jesus love me?"

My response is simple: "He will love you the same way He loved me!"

Only I know the old Marc. Only I know how putrid my thoughts have been, the motives behind my past decisions, and yet He still loves me. He still pursues me. He still calls me. And because I know what God redeemed me from, I am motivated to do my all to reach others with the same grace He's shown me.

In fact, one of the most incredible passages in relation to God wanting us to use our story is found in the last pages of God's Holy Word. John writes in Revelation 12:11 (NKJV), "And they overcame him by the blood of the Lamb, and by the word of their testimony." Did you get the thrust of the passage? The Lord speaks of "overcoming" the Great Dragon (Satan) with the blood of the Lamb, which I get. But then He drops this bombshell of something that doesn't seem to belong in that same train of thought: "And by the word of their testimony." Did God just place Jesus's precious blood in the same context as our testimony? You see, when God is lifted high, when we share the testimony of our failures and His goodness, He says, "I 'will draw all peoples to Myself'" (John 12:32, NKJV). God can use your story, your failures, and your testimony. In fact, He wants to.

When I speak to people about evangelism, in light of their failures, most will admit not leading others to the Lord has been of paramount concern. They have felt the nudging but suppressed it time and again. They have even felt the shame of not having followed through with God's subtle prompting. But if that is so, why don't more people just take a chance and go for it? In a word: fear—fear of the unknown, fear of messing up, fear of being asked a question they can't answer. In fact, the most referred-to fear relates to not knowing enough to share Jesus.

First, we must understand that fear is not something God has given us. In fact, through His precious sacrifice, we are endued with the full power of the Holy Spirit to overcome such fear. He said, "For God has not given us a spirit of fear, but of power and of love and of a sound mind" (2 Timothy 1:7, NKJV). Fear is of the enemy, and it becomes a clear tactic within Satan's modus operandi as he builds the moment up to an unattainable objective. If he can convince us to live in fear, we become a part of the staggering statistic of yet another believer who will not share his or her faith.

Secondly, it's important to note that our only potential to fail is founded in *not* telling others about Jesus in the first place. As for the main mental block, not knowing enough of the Bible, I like to site the testimony of the man in the Scriptures who was blind from his birth. Don't get me wrong—it's imperative we know and apply the Word, but we can't use that as our universal cop-out when God presents an opportunity to share Jesus!

In chapter 9 of John's Gospel (NKJV), Jesus and his disciples came across a man, who the Bible states "was blind from his birth." His disciples asked the common question of the day: "Who sinned, this man or his parents, that he was born blind?" (v. 2). You see, they preferred to assign blame than get to know the man or hear his story. Sound familiar?

Unfortunately, we are not so different today. After Jesus healed this young man, the ones who witnessed this miraculous act, including the religious leaders, began to demand answers. The common perception of his healing was trickery, sleight of hand, and perhaps mistaken identity. But through all the faithless probing, and the coolest part of this narrative is what the healed man did not say. He did not quote scripture. He did not cite the Torah. He did not stand up and wax eloquent concerning the said miracle as if to explain the supernatural act. And he did not hide behind what he did not know, which was everything! He simply spoke truth. Truth that was evident. His timely retort still stands firm today: "I don't know much of anything about Jesus or what He is, but 'one thing I know: that though I was blind, now I see'" (v.25).

After the mic-drop, the Pharisees tried to argue Jesus's identity, and rather than pressing this unlearned man into the corner, he began to teach them.

> The man answered and said to them, "Why, this is a marvelous thing, that you do not know where He is from; yet He has opened my eyes! Now we know God does not hear sinners; but if anyone is a worshiper of God and does His will, He hears them. Since the world began it has been unheard of that anyone opened the eyes of one who was blind. If this Man were not from God, He could do nothing." They answered and said to him, "You were completely born in sins, and you are teaching us?" And they cast him out. (John 9:30–34)

You see, it's rarely about how much you know or feel you don't know; it's more often about being willing to submit to the Holy Spirit's move in the moment. And like the blind man, you shouldn't try to overcompensate, over-talk, or over-spiritualize but simply use your failures, your lack of understanding, and your helplessness and speak truth. That's a tough proposition with which to argue! So, commit to throw all inhibitions to the wind, and use your failures.

7

TIME IS OF THE ESSENCE

The very word RUSH triggers the idea of being expedient about something. In the case of our RUSH Ministries mandate, "Reaching the Unchurched," time *is* of the essence, to reach people before it is everlasting too late! According to statistics, approximately 4.5 billion people in the world are unsaved and 1 billion have never heard the Gospel of Jesus Christ! I would say that alone constitutes a RUSH to get the message of Jesus out to the masses. You may be skeptical like I was. After all, how can there be anyone who has not heard the Gospel message with the internet, media, and such sophisticated technology? I know that it may be hard to swallow, but there may even be some of those people right next door.

In David Platt's book, *Radical*, Platt asserts "If we look at the progression of how people are saved as read from Romans 10:13ff, we see one potential breakdown. First, let's look at God's divine plan for the redemption of mankind, since 'all have rejected God' already." He points out,

> God sends His servants > His servants preach > People hear > Hearers believe > Believers call > Everyone who calls is saved.

Platt concludes by asking the simple question: "Is there any place where this plan can breakdown?" He answers:

> Obviously, everyone who calls on the name of the Lord will be saved. No breakdown there. Everyone who believes will call. Many who hear (not all, but many) will believe. People will hear the gospel when we preach it to them. And God is most definitely still in the business of sending His servants. That means there is only one potential breakdown in this progression—when servants of God do not preach the gospel to all people.

So, are you? Are you preaching the Gospel? Are you sharing the message of hope with the world? Are you meeting them where they are? Are you using your failures? If you're like most Christians, you want to, and perhaps you will at the "right" time. However, the reality is *time* is something you do not have. The thought you've just had, the words you've just spoken, the person you've just passed in the hall, is a fleeting moment, a lost moment, an opportunity gone by. Too heavy? It should be! I think more needs to be said about the fact that there is a RUSH to get the message of Jesus to every nation, tongue, and kindred.

Again, if the mortality rate is 163,898 per day, then each day, another multitude of people are lost forever, perhaps never hearing the Gospel message. That's approximately 6,829 per hour, 114 people per minute, nearly 2 per second. And a heavy percentage are not believers! That is not okay with me. It is not okay with Jesus, who came that "any should perish but that all should come to repentance" (2 Peter 3:9, NKJV). God, help us. God, help *me* to pursue those who are much like those orphan boys that day, outside of the gate of redemption. Holy Spirit remind us all daily to reach through the gate and share our own story.

Here's the deal. The one luxury we do not have is time. We must make the most of every second. This is true in our relationships and in our evangelistic efforts. Lives are at stake! Paul charges the church in Ephesus and us today, "See then that ye walk circumspectly, not as fools, but as wise, *redeeming the time*, because the days are evil" (Ephesians 5:15–16, KJV, emphasis mine).

In this passage, I first want to focus on the phrase "redeeming the time." The literal meaning here is "to make most of the time you have," to "cash in the right-now moments" of our life. What would the world look like if the Christian population were redeeming the time? What would your town look like if your church congregation, your youth group, redeemed the time? What would your faith walk look like if *you* redeemed the time? I submit to you, everything would change. Not only would more people come to know Christ because we Christians made better use of time given, but I also believe we would walk less offended by others and become more focused on the prize—namely, Jesus.

Next, the charge for us to "walk circumspectly" is a very interesting thought. Perhaps a slightly different look will shed some light on the meaning. I have enjoyed deer hunting as a boy, as a dad taking my own children on hunts, and most recently, as a grandfather, I have the privilege of taking my grands hunting. But it was my years in the military that this passage truly came alive for me for first time. In the army, we were taught to be at one with our surroundings. This is true for the art of camouflage, noticing traps set by enemy forces, and most importantly, not exposing yourself to the enemy. When I understood this concept through my training, I noticed something different about the deer I had been hunting all the previous years. The smaller, less-seasoned deer would traipse aimlessly into an open field or cross a break in the covering, completely unaware of the present danger that awaited him. In stark contrast, the older, more mature bucks, with large antlers, are rarely seen in the open. In fact, one day while hunting and enjoying the wondrous beauty of God's creation (I do less "hunting" and more praising God in the woods these days), a large, mature buck stepped into view. There he was, the big boy I'd been hunting for two years (that's a South Georgia euphemism for a trophy buck). But this time, something was different. Almost immediately, all my training, all the animal shows on Discovery, the deer-hunting tactics, coupled with the passage in Ephesians 5, all mingled together. I watched this seasoned buck walking to the edge of a clearing, and he was walking circumspectly. His steps seemed calculatedly robotic. He would pick up his leg and freeze mid-step. He would listen and then carefully place his foot. He would take another step, pause again, and then lift his nose to the wind, filtering out any unknowing smells. I thought, *How informed this mature buck seems, as if he knows something is there, waiting to take him out.*

Before I could get a shot off, he picked up my scent in the shifting wind and bolted out of sight. He was safe to live another day, for another hunt. As I thought over and over of my own blunders, it occurred to me, *Well, that ol' buck didn't get that mature from being careless!* No, sir. He had learned to walk *circumspectly.* Each day could be his last as deer hunters and predators sought to take his life. Each moment, each second, he lived was a success—at least to him.

God, help me to consider the enemy who stands in wait "to steal, kill, and destroy" (John 10:10a, KJV). Help me to walk circumspectly and not at all carelessly through this life. Help me to redeem the time and be sensitive to the lost and the needs of the broken. After all, time is precious and the souls we must reach are even more precious. Time *is* of the essence. Don't miss it! In fact, let us RUSH at the chance to share the hope of the world with a bankrupt soul.

As I think on, moving forward with intentionality, I offer up this thought. Virtually every decision we've ever made hinged on a moment of decision, some more time sensitive than others. However, all our decisions in life hinge on right-now moments. After all, you are not promised another second in life. James dealt with such delayed action this way.

Come now, you who say, "Today or tomorrow we will go to such and such a city, spend a year there, buy and sell, and make a profit"; whereas you do not know what will happen tomorrow. For what is your life? It is even a vapor that appears for a little time and then vanishes away. Instead you ought to say, "If the Lord wills, we shall live and do this or that." But now you boast in your arrogance. All such boasting is evil. Therefore, to him who knows to do good and does not do it, to him it is sin. (James 4:13–7, NKJV).

When I read that, it seems we are being a little pretentious to believe we can postpone anything God has clearly prompted us to do. Sharing our faith is not up in the air for debate. God has clearly given us our mandate, our commission to tell the world. And you can't just put it off because it's not in your timeline of today's to-do list. The time is now. Time is of the essence.

8

COMMISSION OR PRIVILEGE?

You can find the Great Commission in at least five different places, in each of the four Gospels and then again in Acts 1:8. Jesus, in His final words before the ascension, charging His followers gathered and us today to "go," to "baptize," to "make disciples of all people." Why, then, do we believers seem to spend so much time "trying to find God's will" for our life. Could it be any clearer why you were placed on earth? Even in the early remarks from Elohim God in Genesis, our Creator says, "be fruitful and multiply" (Genesis 1:28, NKJV).

I know, if you're like most of us, we have our own perception of what that means! But what we are really doing is what most seminary students learn in their first semester of hermeneutics (the science/art of biblical interpretation), we are practicing *eisegesis*. Without getting into a deep theological discussion, simply put, eisegesis is reading Scripture and asking, "What does it mean to me?" It's when the reader imposes his or her philosophy, dogma, or opinion into the interpretation of the text.

Conversely, *exegesis* is drawing out text's meaning in accordance with the author's context and discoverable meaning. This is the proper method of interpretation. Can I say this in a kind, pastoral manner: "It doesn't matter what the text "means to you" but rather what God meant when He moved over the human writers, as they penned His Holy Word.

I have been told that if Scripture contains a truth one time, it's important. Two times, pay close attention. More than that, just do it! And here, at least five times, directly in the commission, Jesus told us to go. What more is there to understand? What else can that possibly mean? But there's more.

God told us to "be fruitful and multiply." What is our "fruit"? What are we to make more of? As previously stated, the Bible mentions Christian only twice and disciple more than 270 times. It is clear what God is saying. As you pay closer attention to the word "fruitful," and you will see the obvious root word, "fruit" to imply bearing fruit. As we look into the New Testament, Jesus teaches more on bearing fruit, and once again, we see the simplicity. It is talking about replicating that which is in you and birthing forth more of the same kind. With reaching the unchurched for Christ, the same is true. As a child of God and a follower of Jesus Christ, we are His disciples. If you're wondering how Jesus measured discipleship, he based it on our "love one for another." Jesus said, "By this all will know that you are My disciples, if you have love for one another" (John 13:35, NKJV).

As a Christ follower, we are to love others, and through the lenses of love, we see people who need Jesus, and we should have a desire for them to know His redemptive plan. Subsequently, the fruit we will bear is more followers of Christ with the same heart to go, to teach, to love, to disciple, and to make more disciples—hence, bearing fruit.

I feel confident that as you read this book, your spirit will receive the nudging you should be reaching the world with the message of the blessed gospel. But I want to impart a simple yet profound thought that may change your life. It did mine.

The commission from Jesus has been interpreted by evangelical Christians as meaning that his followers have the *duty* to *go*, *teach*, and *baptize*. Although the command was initially given directly only to Christ's apostles and those in the immediate crowd, evangelical Christian theology has typically interpreted the commission as a directive to all Christians of every time and place. However, it is unknown who first coined the term the Great Commission. Scholars such as Eduard Riggenbach (in *Der Trinitarische Taufbefel*) and J. H. Oldham et al. (in *The Missionary Motive*) assert the very phraseology did not exist until after the year 1650. And so, it seems to be the word commission that brings some of us to a grinding halt. Perhaps the thoughts of "duty" or "responsibility" come to mind and the subsequent feeling of "have to" rubs many the wrong way. After all, shouldn't being a witness for Jesus be laced with freedom and liberty? So it seems. But if that's true, then maybe God intends us to grow into a fruitful Christian who can shift from the concept of duty, "I have to go", to the concept of "I get to go"!

Let's look at it this way. When Stephanie had our first child, Tyler, and then our second, Ashli Marie, a couple of years later, I realized another concept of reproducing, procreating, or being fruitful. The joy that comes from bringing forth something out of yourself, from your own seed, is immeasurable! According to Psalm 127:3 (NKJV), "Children are an heritage of the LORD: and the fruit of the womb is his reward."

I want to bring your attention to this idea of reward. You and I are rewarded with offspring or "fruit of the womb." Fruit of our spiritual labors should be viewed as a reward, as well! We need only be reminded of this truth because too often, evangelism feels like a commissionable chore rather than a rewarded privilege. Not sharing our faith may be something we feel guilty about, so we reluctantly agree to go. But if we merely "go" out of duty, our going will more than likely be short-lived and at best non-fulfilling as a Christian. However, it is my intent that you see evangelism the way God sees it—as part of your purpose in this world, a reward He graciously brings you into. You don't *have* to go. You *get* to!

To evangelize someone is to tell them the good news! It is to share with them the message of a hope found in a personal relationship with God, through His son, Jesus.

I think when we truly understand the concept of "get to" as the message of telling people of God's good news, it sounds a lot more like a divine privilege and a lot less like a churchy chore! In fact, I believe the greatest privilege in this life is just that: sharing Jesus with another. To see a person respond and receive eternal life through the finished work of the cross should be seen as a supernatural act going from death to life. And that should get us excited. So, to end where we began, "Will *you* go?" And if you will go, will you go for all people, the orphaned, the ones on the outside, the unchurched? Will you reach through the gate?

I will.

9

DO IT ANYWAY!

Will you throw all inhibitions to the wind? Will you step into the greatest privilege in this life, to see another come to life in Christ? I hope so. But if there's any leftover reserve, just do it anyway. Sounding a little cynical? Maybe so.

"Do it anyway" may like the title to a great country song, Huh? Well, that's because it is an excerpt from a Martina McBride song, entitled, "Anyway." The premise of the song is much like that of this chapter. In fact, the lyrics have a direct similarity to that of *The Paradoxical Commandments*, written by Dr. Kent M. Keith:

> People are illogical, unreasonable, and self-centered.
> *Love them anyway.*
> If you do good, people will accuse you of selfish ulterior motives.
> *Do good anyway.*
> If you are successful, you will win false friends and true enemies.
> *Succeed anyway.*
> The good you do today will be forgotten tomorrow.
> *Do good anyway.*
> Honesty and frankness make you

vulnerable.
Be honest and frank anyway.
The biggest men and women with the
biggest ideas can be shot down by the
smallest men and women with the smallest minds.
Think big anyway.
People favor underdogs but follow only top dogs.
Fight for a few underdogs anyway.
What you spend years building may be
destroyed overnight.
Build anyway.
People really need help but may attack you if you
do help them.
Help people anyway.
Give the world the best you have and
you'll get kicked in the teeth.
Give the world the best you have anyway.
(© Copyright Kent M. Keith 1968, renewed 2001)

With that, let me warn you—I may become even more cynical as we approach the book's end, especially as it pertains to the naysayers and pessimists out there. It's just that in redeeming the time, I choose not to allow people to dictate my direction or God-given destiny. I prefer to take jabs in stride, always remaining teachable while keeping my eyes on the prize. Jesus is my prize, not man's opinion of me. The true yet harsh reality is people within the church, the "religious" crowd, if you will, can at times become the most condescending and critical. It's a little too ironic: the very people who should be encouraging you to reach into the unchurched community can become the very ones who say, "You don't want those kids in here" or "You are just doing that to get a name for yourself."

Despite this, I say, "Dare to dream, dare to build up, dare to think big, and dare to do it anyway!" Let them talk, but don't let them distract you from your calling to go.

The price of God's favor is you won't be liked by everyone! In fact, God's anointing can immediately usher in the attacks and opposition of antagonist and haters! And hear me, God may move many obstacles out of our path, but He rarely moves the oppositions. However, if God is on the throne of your life, He will render those oppositions powerless over you, reminding you to whom all glory is due.

But let's take it one step further in regard to God's anointing over our life. I've realized that our work for the Lord cannot be relegated to simple giftedness, talents, or traits you innately possess. Our evangelism efforts still must be driven by God's anointing upon your life. And while that is something we all should desire, consider the anointing of His presence. In Scripture, the oil is symbolic of the Spirit of God and specifically the presence of the Holy Spirit. But I'm reminded of the process from which the oil is extracted, through crushing or pressing of the olives. I feel the same is true for you and me. To have the truest and purest presence of the Holy Spirit's control over our life, and flowing through us, we too must be crushed. Are you willing to accept that proposition? It will be tough but invite the crushing anyway.

I know that this seems a little on the side of negativity or even a little paradoxical itself for a pastor to say this, but we must also repel the idea this will be easy. The truth is, I have personally been targeted by churches, by pastors, and even people within my own family and ministry. But as Jesus told His disciples, there are times you must "shake the dust off your feet" (Matthew 10:15, KJV), which is to say, don't take it personally; just carry on with your mission. Dare to do it anyway. I'm reminded of how Jesus took an intentional step outside the religious crowd of the day to surround Himself with the unchurched crowd. He rebuked religiosity and the leaders who propagated a message of self-righteous behavior. He scolded them with the most aggressive of rebukes. He said to them,

> Woe to you, scribes and Pharisees, hypocrites! For you are like whitewashed tombs which indeed appear beautiful outwardly, but inside are full of dead men's bones and all uncleanness. (Matthew 23:27, NKJV)

They must have looked quite fancy with their clothing and stoic mannerisms, and they looked down on common people as dumb sheep. But, if Jesus is the Great Shepherd, I'll take the compliment of being a sheep any day! I'm convinced there's much to be learned and applied to today's religious culture as well. It is my experience, many of the mightiest warriors for Jesus are those who were unchurched and were found outside the gate.

I feel it imperative to bring this out in the open because if you are reading this book, you already have a burden for the lost. Think about this: Jesus did the exact opposite from what most of us do today to build a church. He went away from and even rebuked the religious crowd of the day. He sought after the common fisherman, the tax collectors, and even the lepers, perhaps the most-avoided people group in the land in which Jesus lived, as if to say, "Everyone can be a part." It was as if Jesus was saying, "I don't need your religious presuppositions. I just want a heart willing to love the ones on the outside. Don't worry about recruiting followers of your dreams. Just surround yourself with those passionately pursuing Me and those with a heart to win the lost. They will run the race with you."

Not all the others will agree, but *run the race anyway*.

Wait a minute, Marc. Are you saying *not* to have anything to do with the church? I am not saying that at all. However, I am saying to prepare yourself for the moment when people you trust within the church or religious community, judge you more harshly for wanting to bring in the poor, hurting, broken, and unchurched crowd. It happened with Jesus, and it will with you. If you expect this, you will not be paralyzed when it *does* happen. It will still break your heart to see people you thought loved the Lord and wanted to see people reached with the glorious Gospel, come at you with pistols blazing! The truth is though, as we read Scripture, we should anticipate this kind of reaction. Thank God for the group of people I serve with today at NorthRidge Church. They genuinely want all people to come into our church. For that, I am most thankful!

Like any other visionary, strategist, or leader, this personal attack has come my way too. Sitting across the table and listening to someone attacking your character, integrity, and motives simply breaks your heart. Not for you but for them. They represent the same crowd that Jesus often wrestled with in the Pharisaical community. How did Jesus react to them? By calling them "hypocrites." And as we've already cited, Jesus spoke vehemently to the religious crowd of His day: "Woe to you."

Harsh and even defaming sorrows spoken over them from a loving savior. But even Jesus had very little patience for the absurdity of one seeing him or herself as better than another. And I concur. As you go, be ready for the dirty, broken, and disenfranchised to walk through the doors of your church. Will you treat them different? Or will you honor the broken prostitute when she shows up for worship, in the same manner in which you treat the millionaire?

That said, how does this effect you when reaching the unchurched, the spiritually orphaned? Knowing you will be placing yourself under such scrutiny is a big part of combating it when it comes. Ultimately, Jesus, through His sovereignty, chose to partner with common people, with whom the religious community would have never given a second look. Let us never stereotype a group of people, even the religious community. Everyone deserves a fair shake!

I was fortunate to have been mentored by some incredible men and women of God, including previous pastors and those God has more recently put in my life. But to simply assume that all pastors, church members, and so on will embrace the mission to reach the unchurched will set you up for deep hurt. It does me well to consider again the words the conference leader spoke to me on that pivotal day: "You don't want that kind in here; they're trouble." In light of all the scrutiny, the personal attacks, the murmuring, and even the in-your-face cruelty, dare to *reach out anyway*!

It is worth it. Regardless of the venue in which I have spoken—whether a funeral, a wedding, a youth meeting, a conference, or a third-world country—I have literally seen thousands of people come to Christ. Why? Because I have given them the opportunity to know the greatest hope, the greatest love, the only answer to all the world's problems, the person of Jesus Christ!

Reach through the gate. See the lost, the forgotten, the undone, and even the ones who couldn't be a part of the assemblage that day, the orphans outside both the figurative and the literal gate. Dare to reach the unchurched. Dare to invite the ones who look different. As I stated earlier, they will change the course of history. And when you become weary in the work, broken from attacks on your motives and criticism from even those you love and respect, remember, Jesus understands. He doesn't offer an out but rather expects you to persevere for the glory of God.

He says to us, "Do it anyway."

CONCLUSION: AND THEN THERE WAS "JACK"

What kind of book would this be without a proper real-life application? Not much, I suppose. That's why I want to conclude with the story of Jack, as we will call him.

There we were, in the mission field yet again. We'd been there a hundred times, or at least it seemed. It was June 2015, and we had brought another team of short-term missionaries to a beautiful island in the Caribbean. We would work hard, feed some very needy people, minister in song, and who knows? Maybe many would accept Christ. It seemed simple enough. After all, because of my past trips, I knew exactly what to expect. But this trip would forever change our life.

On the second day of the trip, we took the team into the heart of a very poor, depressed section, which the locals call the "ghetto." Because many mission teams avoided this area, we found it somewhat of an untapped well in the field of evangelism. We had prepared hundreds of hotdogs and cups of fruit punch, and we were off to feed the *least of these*. After a few moments of feeding, my wife, Stephanie, noticed one little boy who was being bullied and pushed aside in the feeding line. I guess we had all seen him, but my wife really connected with this boy. My five-foot-four wife stepped from behind our serving table and made a beeline to this little boy. I'd seen that look before, and I, for one, felt sorry for whoever was on the receiving end. *This is about to get interesting*, I thought.

My recollection of the moment was her plowing through those

bullies like a parting of the Red Sea. She recalls it in a much more passive manner. I digress. Either way, as she approached the boy, she greeted him with a discreet side-hug. She said confidently but humbly, "Come with me."

As Stephanie and this boy approached the table, more of his issues came into full view. He was frail. He had open wounds on his shins and feet from catching crab in the surf. I remember what he was wearing—a pair of women's shorts at least three sizes too big, tied together at the waist with a burlap string. His shirt was a men's shirt, conversely two sizes too small, held together with two or three buttons, each fastened out of its place. He wore a pair of tattered red flip-flops, and his relatively large feet dragged on the ground, creating the worst calluses I had ever seen on one's heels. But what I remember most, what still moves me today, was the darkness of his eyes. He appeared to have no hope. He had the emptiest look on his face, a blankness that permeated from within his soul and showed through his eyes.

Stephanie began to hand him one hotdog, then another, but instead of eating them, he grabbed them quickly and pressed them inside his utterly soiled clothing, and against his filthy body.

"No, no, son, you don't have to do that!" Stephanie urged. "There's plenty of food here for you."

But the young man's retort, while looking down at the ground in embarrassment: "Yes, Miss, but I don't know what I will eat tomorrow."

The look on my wife's face spoke a thousand words. I waited for her next move. Emotion filled her eyes. "What's your name, baby?" she asked.

Still looking down, he answered softly, "Jeremy, Miss."

She pressed in. "Jeremy, where do you live?"

He pointed across the creek to a little delapidated structure about eight feet by eight feet. He turned, and we followed him to his house. As we made our way, we traversed a large log that had fallen across the creek, creating a makeshift bridge. Once Jeremy made it to the door of his home, he proceeded to take a key he'd kept from a necklace around his neck (as if anyone would want to break in and steal ... what?). As he opened the door, we looked in and to our horror, we saw what he called home. There, on the dirt floor, lay stack of cardboard boxes, the ones on the bottom drawing water from the earth. This was his bed. To the right, as you entered, was a wheel from on old car, with live coals still underneath and a paint can with rice scraps he had eaten earlier, on the wall of he can. Much to our chagrin, we could still smell fumes from the remnants of the paint.

Stephanie was mortified. She began to weep openly. I too felt the anguish for this little fella. But what could we do? Some of our team had also made it over to the house, and they were watching intently to see how we handled the moment. I quickly grabbed Stephanie and pulled her behind a large tree to help her regain her composure. After all, we were the leaders. We had to save face. It's not like we hadn't seen tough situations before that moment.

I spoke sternly but respectfully to my wife, "Steph, we've got to pull it together. We've seen this before. We are leading a team. We cannot let them see us this way!"

You see, we always tell our teams, "Don't allow yourself to get so moved that you lose sight of the short time you have to change lives."

Stephanie looked at me, tears streaming down her face. "Marc, I can't leave this little boy here. We've got to take him with us!"

Now I was past the point of losing it. I'd seen this in my bride before. She doesn't easily cave when she's compelled in such a manner.

"Stephanie, you've got to pull yourself together! We can't just throw this kid on the bus and take him home. He's not a puppy. He's a child. There are laws against this sort of thing. You may have heard of it. It's called kidnapping!"

I felt sure after that loving reminder, she would understand. Boy, was I wrong. It was me who was about to learn a lesson about my wife and her heart for truly reaching the world.

My sweet, but firm spoken wife looked up at me with a stern, and convincing manner. "Marc, we've prayed for years about starting an orphanage." I nodded in affirmation. "Before we can ever have an orphanage and hope to save the multitudes, we've got to be prepared to save just *one*."

And not at all disrespectfully, she raised one finger as if to represent all the "ones" out there beyond the gate. I melted in my disappointment in myself. I realized she was right. We had come for them, for the "ones" no one wanted.

And there stood our one.

After we spoke to the community elders, we got permission to take this little boy with us to the hotel to get him fed, clothed, and cared for properly. While there, we learned of his age and other telling information. He thought himself to be around thirteen, but much to his displeasure, he later found out he was only twelve. Once we located his birth certificate, we also realized his name was not Jeremy but in fact was Jack. So why did he go by Jeremy all this time? If you know the Jamaican dialect, Jeremy is actually pronounced more like "Germy." We later discovered that's exactly what the locals were calling this little orphaned street kid. They nicknamed him "Germy" because "he was always smelly and dirty," they explained. How cruel! And if that wasn't bad enough, we discovered this little boy had been abandoned and fending for himself since age seven. Of course there were stents of foster care or homes, but Jeremy was a runner. He always made it back to the streets. To add insult to injury, once back in the streets, instead of offering him aid, the locals pushed him aside and called him "Germy". So, Jack grew up thinking they were calling him Jeremy, and that's the name he knew.

It was now up to Stephanie and me. We only had a couple of choices. Would we pass this off as too hard? Or would we find him a place to stay there? Surely, someone would step up. Unfortunately, at that time, neither of the two options would suffice. There was no one. "Street boys," as they were called, had already built for themselves quite the reputation. The locals saw them as thieves, liars, and due to countless other acts that made them an unwanted group of people, the children were cast aways from society. However, simply avoiding this task because it was too difficult was not in our character. And Jack—or Jeremy, as he wanted to be called—had no one who could offer him care there. Both his mother and father were not able to be a part of his life, as they couldn't even care for themselves, much less a child.

We were the ones. Stephanie and I were handpicked by God to rescue this little boy. After everyone in the government told us the unlikelihood of the US embassy offering Jeremy a visa, we were more inclined to pray like never before. So, after several thousands of dollars, much time, fervent prayer, and against all odds, we were finally scheduled for our Embassy interview that would decide Jeremy's fate. All of his future would ride on this one person in the interview window and that five minute interview with him/her. But as God's grace had gone before us, when we made our way over to the interview window, there stood a confident, but humble woman of God. She couldn't have been over 25 years old. But she saw what many others couldn't. She saw the moment as one of God's Divine appointments where her decision could save or condemn this little boy's life. On that day, and because of much prayer and His amazing grace, we were approved to bring Jeremy home with us. We got approval for a school visa, so Jeremy could go to school in the United States. We had accepted the call of God not only to "go" but to keep going and to live out the Gospel in this depraved, broken, and forgotten little boy.

Looking back now, I can't even fathom how God made it possible, but He knew the years of travelling to this island had actually prepared us for an encounter with the least of these. There's so much I could say about this journey with Jeremy, which is still ongoing and probably will be until God calls us home. But there is one thing I do want to mention in this book, and perhaps this will serve as precursor to my next book, and that is Jeremy's eternal hope. You see, that's the real reason for our encounter. And that's the real reason for this book.

When we brought Jeremy into our home, we committed to love him like our own son. My wife knew this before me, but I soon caught on. At night, we would go in a pray for him, and he would snarl, grunt, and cry uncontrollably. I am convinced Jeremy was either under severe demonic oppression, influence, or perhaps even possession. Our first steps were to save him in the physical, but God knew what Jeremy needed in the spiritual. He needed to be delivered! He needed to be introduced to a loving Savior who would also adopt him as His own.

A few months after loving this little boy like our own child, we saw the real reason for this rescue. One Sunday, I was preaching, like every other Sunday, and at the end of the service (not really at the "right" time, mind you; I hadn't given the formal, "simple" invitation), Jeremy got up from his seat from the back row. He walked confidently down the aisle like a bride adorned in the purest of white gowns, making her way to her groom. I can still see this now healthy, strapping young man, dressed in nice clothing as he made his way to Jesus. He had friends, a church family that loved him. Immediately, I was taken back to the moment when Stephanie first brought him through the food line that day. His head was held low. His clothing was tattered. He had no identity, no hope, not even a real name or birthdate. He lacked any level of confidence. But today, his walk was different! He held his head high as he stepped in front of the entire congregation. He walked up to me on the stage.

"Pastor Marc, I want to be saved."

At that moment, I knew. I told him.

"Jeremy, You are no longer an orphan."

God had reached through the gate of Jeremy's economic disparity, his unwantedness, and made him a son of the King! In that very moment, everything he would ever do would be different. His decisions would now be tempered through the grace of Almighty God. Jeremy now walked as a child of the King! I wish I could tell you Jeremy became everything he is supposed to be in life. However, just like you and me, he strives, he struggles, and he misses the mark over and again. The difference now is that he doesn't have to go at it alone. His status has changed. His relationship changed. Therefore, his eternity has changed.

In addition to the working progress in Jeremy's life, everything changed for us through this ordeal—for the good. There would be no more left behind, no more pushed aside. In that millisecond, I thought, *Everyone matters to God, and they'd better start mattering to His Church.* Maybe we'd passed a thousand like Jeremy. But today, we saw the glory of God deposited into the life of this hopeless young man. And that's why we are here. James 1:27 (NKJV) says, "Pure and undefiled religion before God and the Father is this: to visit orphans and widows in their trouble, and to keep oneself unspotted from the world." That's God's heart. It's our mandate.

So, I urge you to *go*, and when you decide to go, *keep on going! Reach the world.* And if it seems like too much of a task, just accept the loving rebuke Stephanie gave me. "You can't reach the world until you're willing to reach just one." For us, it was Jack. *Who's your one* standing in wait? Who is waiting on you to walk by the gate? Will you keep walking or will you reach *through the gate*?

I did.

We love you Jeremy.

BOOK TESTIMONIALS

"The simple steps covered in this book are laced with down-to-earth, passionate, and real-to-life application. Marc Pritchett has simplified the complexities of reaching those far from God. This is a must-read!"

—David Crowder, Crowder Music,
Passion Conferences

"Marc Pritchett has nailed this one! *Through the Gate* has made simple the art of Personal Evangelism. I've been a partner with Marc's ministry for many years, and He is the real deal. This one is a must-read!"

—Eddie Carswell, Founder of Winter
Jam Tour, Newsong Co-Founder

"The church is the only organization that exists for non-members! Marc Pritchett nails it in *Through the Gate!* It is not about us in the church but those outside of it! I hope every church in America gets this book! Mine sure will!"

—*Dr. Benny Tate, Senior Pastor,*
Rock Springs Church

"An absolute necessary read! As our culture spins out of control and the world moves toward a godless society, the passion, power, and presentation of the Gospel is essential in these trying times. Marc Pritchett's *Through the Gate* creates a simple and clear path for personal evangelism to reach those who have been blinded by this age."

—*Ray Flynn, President and CEO,*
Abraham Productions, Inc.